IN THE
HEART
OF THE
QUAKE

Look for other
DISASTER ZONE books

In the Eye of the Tornado

IN THE HEART OF THE QUAKE

DAVID LEVITHAN

AN
APPLE
PAPERBACK

SCHOLASTIC INC.
New York Toronto London Auckland Sydney

ISBN 0-590-12916-3

12 11 10 9 8 7 6 5 4 3   1 2 3/0

Printed in the U.S.A.   40

First Scholastic printing, May 1998

For Cary
(who can be found in many of these sentences)

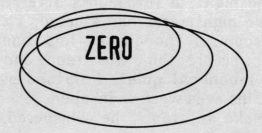

ZERO

My brother can't sleep.

The earthquakes keep him awake.

Buildings collapse. People are trapped screaming. Sidewalks rise and crash like waves.

His bed doesn't move.

It's all in his mind.

My brother, Stieg, has the Sense. It's been in our family for generations. It provides a view of the future. It tells of disasters yet to come.

And right now it is yelling *earthquake*.

But it won't say when. And it won't say where.

We've given Stieg warm milk and extra pillows. We've given him sleeping medicine.

It doesn't matter.

The Sense will not be ignored.

I can hear him from my bed. I can hear him pounding the walls with his fists. He cries out in fear. He cries out in frustration.

There's nothing I can do.

One night, a few nights after the earthquake nightmares had started, I crept into his room. I thought he had finally found sleep. His breathing was steady and the room was moonlight quiet. I tiptoed over to his bed. His eyes were wide-open.

"Make it stop," he whispered. "Please make it stop."

We had just been through a tornado. We had saved lives. Saving lives was why Stieg had been given the Sense. He knew this. He just wasn't ready for its darker side.

It hit him when he least expected it. He lost his balance. He thought the ground was moving.

He would tell me what it was like. I would write it down in our Atwood Family Chronicles. Together, we searched his dreams for clues. We sifted through the mystery to find the where and the when.

He saw a girl's doll sitting atop an anonymous pile of wreckage. As he passed, the doll winked.

He heard sobs and cries for help. He smelled fire and gas.

Most of all, he felt the ground move. He felt himself falling. There was nothing he could do to steady himself. He always fell. And then the roof collapsed. And then the beam pinned him to the floor. And then a steeple crashed down onto passing cars.

All the time, he heard screams.

When he woke up, the screams wouldn't go away.

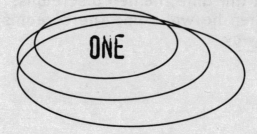

ONE

We weren't even in our own house. It wasn't safe to go back there. Not yet.

In some strange way, Stieg and I were fugitives. We were wanted by the government — by Agent James Taggart of Operation Secret Storm, to be exact. He knew about the Sense. He had used my father's Sense for the government's own purposes.

My parents both died on one of Taggart's missions, two years ago.

Taggart wanted Stieg and me to take their places.

To which we said: *No way*.

But Taggart didn't like to take no for an answer. He'd tried to catch us in Kenmore, Kansas, the town where we'd fought the tornado. And now he had our house and our grandfather under surveillance. We didn't think there was anything he could do (legally). But we weren't going to go back until we were one hundred percent sure.

In the meantime, we were staying in the apartment of Marty Chester, on Sixteenth Street in Washington, D.C. Marty was a congressional aide. My parents had saved his parents from a forest fire in the 1960s.(While they were alive, my parents had saved hundreds of people from disasters. Most of these people are now willing to give Stieg and me a helping hand. We call these people the Network.)

Marty was using his contacts in the FBI and the CIA to check out Taggart. In the meantime, our grandfather (our mother's father, with whom we live) was mobilizing other members of the Network to guarantee our safety, if they could. There were ways we could get into Grandfather's house unnoticed, but once we got in there, we'd be trapped.

Since we were supposed to be lying low, Stieg and I spent most of the day in Marty's apartment. Stieg watched endless amounts of TV. I tried to get him to take naps, but he was clearly afraid of sleep. (He'd never admit to it; I just knew.)

While Stieg switched channels, I flipped through the Atwood Family Chronicles. The oldest Chronicle dates back to 1843. Ever since then, our family has written about the Sense and its effects. There are dozens of volumes, covering all kinds of disasters. After Stieg had his first earthquake premonition, I asked Grandfather to send me (through intermediaries) the quake-related books.

So there I sat, with more than one hundred years' worth of earthquake observations at my side. After my parents died, I made it my job to keep track of the Chronicles. If Stieg was the one with the Sense, I would be the one with the history. It seemed like an almost fair trade.

I looked to the Chronicles to see if there was any way to help Stieg. I looked to the Chronicles to find out what was going on.

My great-great-grandfather Christopher wrote on April 16, 1906:

I CANNOT hold a teacup. The tea spills all over the table. The other people on the train think I am NERVOUS or maybe just OLD. But I am not. I cannot help it. I stay in my seat because I cannot WALK.

Christopher Atwood was on a train to San Francisco. The night before, the Sense had delivered the first warnings of the Great

Quake of 1906, just days after Christopher had been wracked with volcano premonitions (correctly predicting the eruption of Mount Vesuvius in Italy).

In 1964, when my father was fifteen, he wrote about a disturbing dream he'd had:

I am cold. Very cold. I am in a field of snow. I hear a roar, like ice breaking apart. Only it's not ice. It's the ground. I fall into the snow, and suddenly all sorts of objects are being thrown at me. A car is about to hit me. It bounces in the air, then crashes into a building. I begin to fall into the ground. Deeper and deeper into the ground.

Soon, my grandfather Edward was possessed by a similar dream. In my grandfather's version, ships were thrown into the air, anchors dangling like dead yo-yos. They came toward him from all directions. He fell into the earth.

This is how he predicted the Anchorage earthquake of 1964, the most powerful earthquake in recent American history. In just five minutes, 200,000 megatons of energy were released. That's equal to 200

7

billion tons of TNT, all exploding at once.

Both my father and my grandfather made it to Anchorage in time to save people.

That's the deal. There's always a reason behind the nightmares.

I wanted Stieg to read the Chronicles. I thought that maybe something in them would strike a chord.

But Stieg refused to look at them.

The one time I'd mentioned a detail from the Chronicles (in Alaska, my father had seen the first floor of a movie theater collapse into the ground), the detail found its way into Stieg's nightmares, making them even worse. The movie theater hovered over his head at all times. He would wait for it to fall. And then it did.

Stieg spent some time E-mailing Zach and Rachel Ede, two people we'd met in Kenmore. Rachel is my age (fourteen) and Zach is older (seventeen). (Stieg's eleven.) Rachel has the Sense like Stieg, although in her family it's called the Message. Rachel and Zach's house was destroyed by the twister in Kenmore — a twister that both Stieg and Rachel had foreseen. At first, I hadn't trusted Zach and Rachel — according to the Chronicles, the Ede family has been a rival to our family for decades. But after Zach and Rachel helped us out in Kenmore, I guess I was willing to leave the rivalry in the past

. . . unless something happened to prove me wrong.

Stieg didn't tell either of the Edes about the earthquake nightmares. Vaguely, he asked Rachel if she'd been having any Messages lately. She said no. Although Stieg wouldn't admit it to me, I could tell he was bummed by this. It meant he was alone in his nightmares. All alone.

"Maybe you should tell Rachel," I casually suggested. We'd been in D.C. for a week. I put down the Chronicle I'd been reading and waited for his response. He was no more than ten feet away, but he pretended he hadn't heard me.

"Let it out," I advised him, standing in front of the television set in order to get his full attention.

"Believe me, I'd let it out if I could," he replied, trying to focus on the TV, even though I was blocking it.

I didn't move. I studied the dark blotches under his eyes. I noted the paleness of his skin. I tried to remember the last time he'd made a joke.

"Stop looking at me!" Stieg yelled, jumping up from the couch.

"What?" I asked. I'd heard him, but "What?" still seemed to be the best response. It felt like I'd been slapped.

"Stop looking at me. Stop staring at me.

9

Stop waiting for me to say something!" he shouted, pacing now. "Stop looking in on me at night. Stop expecting it to make sense. Stop asking me *what's going on.* Because I don't know, Adam. I don't know. I DON'T KNOW!"

"Calm down," I cautioned. Even as he paced, Stieg stumbled.

"Look," he said, his tone way too adult for an eleven-year-old, "I know you wish you were the one with the Sense. *I* wish you were the one with the Sense. Then I could go to sleep. Then I could go home. Then I could be *normal.* I don't care anymore that we saved people's lives. I don't care if the rest of our family saved people's lives. I want it *gone.*"

"Don't say that!" I yelled. "Because it could happen. And then . . ."

"I WANT IT GONE!" Stieg screamed defiantly. "DO YOU HEAR ME? I WANT IT *GONE!*"

Then he stormed out of the room. I heard a door slam. I heard him throw himself on his bed. I expected to hear him cry. But I didn't.

I shut off the TV. Then I turned it back on, since I couldn't stand the silence. I heard a key in the door. Moments later, Marty walked into the apartment.

"What's up?" he asked, friendly enough.

He had no idea.

Loosening his tie, he said, "I have an announcement to make. Where's Stieg?"

"He's sleeping," I lied. "Tell me the news."

Marty smiled.

"I talked to your grandfather," he said. "You can go home."

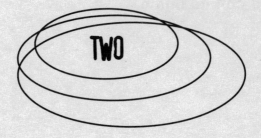

TWO

My grandfather talked to Agent Taggart and his supervisors. He gave them a list of Network members. Senators. Police officers. Lawyers. Judges. Grandfather made it clear: If anything were to happen to me or Stieg, every single person on the list would come down on Taggart so hard that he might not ever stand again. Taggart backed off. He said he'd only wanted to ask us a few questions. He said he'd leave us alone, if that was what Grandfather wanted. He gave his word.

I still expected him to show up at any time.

I didn't trust his word. At all.

Still, we were going home. When I told Stieg, he wouldn't let me see his reaction. But he had to be relieved. I hoped that being home would somehow tame his nightmares. Maybe the familiarity of his bedroom would make things easier.

That's what I hoped.

I was wrong.

We returned home to Connecticut. Sam Nisson, a friend of Grandfather's, picked us up at the airport. The flight between D.C. and Hartford had been short. I had tried to talk to Stieg, but he was ignoring me. He still wanted the Sense to be gone. I didn't want to argue with him.

Grandfather was waiting for us at home. His wheelchair filled the front doorway. Stieg broke out of his gloom and ran for Grandfather with all his might, nearly knocking him back into the hallway with his hug. I looked around the yard for any suspicious cars — Taggart waiting in an unmarked Buick, binoculars tracking our every move. But I couldn't see anything out of the ordinary. Either Taggart had truly left us alone . . . or he was better at hiding than I was at detecting.

As soon as Dr. Nisson left, Grandfather took us down into the Maze. Like most mansions, our house has many secrets — and the Maze is the biggest secret of all. The upstairs area of our house is mirrored in the ground, more or less. The eleven rooms in the Maze

13

are fully equipped with all of the ameni-
ties of upstairs. We have computer screens
that simulate sunlight. We have perfect
TV reception and a kitchen that's even
bigger than the one on the surface. Grandfather, Stieg, and I each have a bedroom
in the Maze. We also have the Nerve Center,
where we can monitor weather conditions
around the world. Or, at least, I can monitor weather conditions around the world —
Stieg couldn't care less, even though he
should.

Before I could go to the Nerve Center and
check out the old coverage of the Kenmore
tornado — as well as any earthquake news of
note — Stieg and I had to sit down with
Grandfather and tell him what had happened.
This took longer than I'd expected — well
into the night. Grandfather is not an Atwood,
so he's never had any firsthand experience
with the Sense. But he'd watched his own
daughter — our mother — deal with our father's Sense. He knows that Stieg possesses
something truly remarkable — something
that must be heeded at all times.

Stieg told Grandfather about the nightmares. Grandfather asked me if there was
anything we could do to help. I picked up one
of the Chronicles and showed him the words
that my other grandfather, my father's fa-

ther, had written as he dreamed of the Anchorage earthquake:

Sometimes I can understand that
this is my mission, and that my nightmares can't compare to the misery
of the real quake. I know how important the Sense is.
But many times I forget. During the
nightmares . . . or when I am awake
and haunted . . . I cannot realize
the Sense's value. I hate the Sense.
I hate my mind. I hate whatever it
is that shows me the earth splitting
and the babies screaming and the anchors swinging in the wind.
But I must overcome this hate. I
must fall willingly into the nightmare and dig for the truth. Because
when I find out, it will be worth it.
I have to believe it will be worth
it.

I flipped the pages. Stieg was looking
away. I read from a later entry, written after the earthquake:

I have to sleep. Even though the
ground still shakes with aftershocks, I have to rest for a moment.

As Marta holds her baby (who I saved?) and as Jonathan helps search through the wreckage, I have to sleep. So I go to the back of the van. I shut my eyes. And I learn: The nightmares are gone. The nightmares led me here. The nightmares saved Marta's baby, and so many others. And now the nightmares have left. I do not miss them. But, like never before, I am glad for them. I had thought they led to death. But really, they led to life.

"*You see?*" I urged Stieg, pushing the Chronicles toward him. *Just take it*, I thought. *Please take it.*

But he wouldn't. He shrank back in his chair. Grandfather put out his hand and gently pushed the book back toward me.

"Not now," he murmured.

"I don't want it," Stieg said to Grandfather, even though he was really talking to me.

"You have to," I argued.

"No," Grandfather said calmly, "he doesn't."

"Don't you care?" I asked both of them.

Stieg shrugged. I wanted to shake him. Hard. He glanced at Grandfather and then smiled at me, triumphant.

"Can I go now?" he asked. Grandfather freed him from the room. He walked steadier as he left . . . until he got to the doorway. Then his legs buckled sharply — he nearly fell. I rose to help him, but he waved me off. He walked to his bedroom without any further trouble.

I turned to Grandfather, hoping he'd seen it all.

"He *can't* give up," I insisted, sitting back down.

"I know," Grandfather replied, nodding.

"So why didn't you say anything to him? How could you just sit there . . . ?" I stopped awkwardly. *How could you just sit there* isn't the best thing to say to someone in a wheelchair. But Grandfather didn't seem to mind.

"This isn't easy for Stieg," he explained. "I think you sometimes forget he's only eleven. You sometimes forget that he's not as strong as you. I know — and you know — that the Sense is a very important thing. But Stieg will have to learn this on his own. He will have to balance the good things about the Sense with the bad things about the Sense. Your grandfather was in his forties when he wrote the entry you just read. It would have been very different if he had been eleven. You are asking Stieg to have an adult's perspective. But he's not an adult yet."

"But he says he wants it to be gone. I'm

afraid that if he believes that strongly enough . . . it *will* disappear," I said.

"Read your books closely," Grandfather advised. "I'll bet most of the people in there wanted the Sense to vanish at one point or another. And I'll tell you what — if I had the power to take it away from Stieg right now, I would. I think it's too much for a child to handle. I'd give it to someone else. If your parents were around . . . well, if they were here, they'd take on the earthquake themselves. I can't do that. I can't do anything about it. But if I could, I would."

"You'd get rid of the Sense, even if it meant that people would die?" I asked.

Grandfather paused for a second. "I'm not sure," he answered. "It's not that easy."

The conversation was going nowhere fast. I needed Grandfather to be my ally. But here he was, taking Stieg's side.

I got up to leave, wishing Grandfather a good night.

"Don't forget you have school tomorrow," he said before I left the room.

I stopped.

I'd forgotten.

School.

18

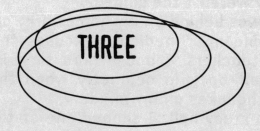

THREE

Even though I'd only been gone for two weeks (one of which was a school vacation), it seemed as if I'd been away for years. The hallways were strangely foreign to me. All of the faces were a blur. I talked to my friends, but it felt like I'd lived a whole life since I last saw them. Obviously, I couldn't tell them what Stieg and I had been doing. Secrecy is key when it comes to the Sense. Not only because of Taggart — we also have to be sure news of the Sense doesn't spread. If it does, Stieg and I would be exposed — and the Sense might disappear, as it had in our family's past.

So instead of telling the truth, I pretended I'd been sick. I had a note in my pocket from Dr. Nisson (Grandfather's friend, Network member) to back me up.

The only person I would have been tempted to tell was my best friend, Jonah. But Jonah had moved to the Midwest, leaving me alone in ninth grade. Sure, I had other friends. But they weren't the same.

I was behind on my homework, and had to fumble my "medical" excuses to each of my teachers. I had a hard time immersing myself back in geometry when there were earthquakes on my mind.

In study hall, I slipped one of the Chronicles out of my backpack and began to read about my great-grandfather Christopher as he approached the San Francisco quake. Ordinarily, I would have been worried that someone would ask me what I was reading. But in the strange hours since I'd been back at school, I'd realized that no one really noticed me. Weirdly, this made me feel safe. Putting geometry completely aside, I looked at my great-grandfather's handwriting from 1906:

April the 17th. The city is calm. I have just arrived. I am in my hotel room. The floor is shifting, but it is ONLY IN MY MIND. How will I tell when the real blast comes? Will I look out the window and actually SEE what I FEEL? I walked through town this evening confused and bewildered. This city is ill-prepared for a tremblor. The buildings are ready to fall.

Then the earthquake hits. The next entry is a long three days later:

I do not know where to begin. I am EXHAUSTED. I have seen horrors I could never have imagined. I am walking in ruins. The city is GONE. It is just a skeleton. The skeleton is falling apart.

But I must go back. I must revisit the first hour. The first seconds. On April 18th, I awoke at four in the morning. The city was absolutely quiet. But I could not sleep. My feeling of FEAR was too GREAT. I did not know what to do. Who could I tell?

With these thoughts in my mind, I left my hotel and began to walk. No one else was awake, except for some patrolmen and an occasional early riser.

I was walking on the street. Suddenly, IT HIT. The whole street was shaken back and forth. Church bells clanged violently. I could not focus. I could barely stand. The street rose up and the ground was turned into WAVES. The whole street lifted and fell like water. Buildings teetered drunkenly. I gasped.

Stones began to fall. Bricks crashed. Chimneys toppled into the streets. I saw one woman look out a window. I saw the chimney above her about to fall. I yelled a warning, but it was too late. It knocked her into the street, headfirst.

Clouds of dust lifted two stories high. Sidewalks crumbled. Windows fell from buildings. Men and women ran into the streets SCREAMING. Streetcars flew from their tracks. The tracks tore from the ground. Some snapped apart and rose in high arcs. Sparks rained down. Electric lines danced on the ground like haywire snakes. A child on the sidewalk was hit by a falling window. I pulled him up. I SAVED him.

Then there was a pause. I looked at his face, which was cut and bleeding. We both took a deep breath. I pulled my handkerchief from my pocket. And then we were BOTH THROWN DOWN. Another tremor hit — this one GREATER THAN THE ONE BEFORE. The street rose and fell higher than my waist. People were prostrated in the streets as bricks fell off the buildings, leaving only shifting frames. Mortar and plaster became instant dust. The noise of buildings falling apart was DEAFENING. Horses made the most horrible sounds. I could not bear it. The dome of the Majestic caved in on itself.

I was PARALYZED while everyone around me YELLED. Buildings were TILTING and WAVERING and even SINKING INTO THE GROUND. I and a few other men dug through the rubble in the street, pulling people out of the debris. We were waiting for the next large tremor, which mercifully did not come. You could still hear the buildings CRASHING. The pillars of City Hall fell all at once.

Every one of those seconds seemed to last a YEAR. I can remember every step I took. I can see the faces of people who ran by. I can see their faces as the buildings fell.

It lasted NO MORE THAN A MINUTE.

Then there was silence. Everyone was in the streets. You would have expected noise. But everyone was silent.

No one could believe it.

The ground had shifted so much that many doors could not open. People were crawling out of windows. People were jumping to escape.

It has ruined many lives. There is NO WATER. There is NO ELECTRICITY.

THE FIRES STILL RAGE.

It is chaos. Complete CHAOS. People run everywhere. There is massive confusion. Nobody knows what to do. Everyone is scared. All order has disintegrated.

I must return outside. There is death and suffering on every corner.

I MUST DO WHAT I CAN.

Sixty-five to seventy-five seconds. That's how long it took to destroy San Francisco. That's how long it took to cause several hundred deaths and more than a thousand injuries.

Sixty-five to seventy-five seconds.

Sitting in study hall, I looked at the clock. I watched as it measured out seventy-five seconds. It seemed to last much longer than a minute. Then I imagined being punched for seventy-five seconds. Being shaken for seventy-five seconds. Being caught in an earthquake for seventy-five seconds.

It would seem like hours and hours.

Was this what Stieg and I were headed for?

The classroom bell rang. I barely heard it. School life — *my* life — seemed very far away. There was only the past of the Chronicles. There was only the future of Stieg's Sense. There were only earthquakes. Impossible to predict . . . without the Sense.

What could we do?

In our town, the middle school and the high school are across the street from each other. I snuck out of school a little early so I could wait for Stieg. I wondered how his day had been.

I wondered if he'd found a way to avoid thinking about earthquakes.

School let out. Kids sprinted from the building, backpacks flying behind them. I searched the crowd for Stieg. After a few minutes, I found him talking to two of his friends — they were exchanging comic books. As Stieg reached out, I could see his hand trembling. The other kids could see it, too. Stieg laughed and made an excuse I couldn't hear. Then he saw me and turned back to his friends, as if I wasn't waiting for him. *Fine*, I thought. I pivoted toward the street, ready to walk home.

Then I heard the yell. Instinctively, I turned around — and saw Stieg right where he'd been, only this time on the ground. He'd fallen backward . . . and from the looks on his friends' faces, I could tell he hadn't been pushed. I rushed over to him, realizing too late that my rushing over was even more embarrassing to him than falling had been. I moved to give Stieg a hand, but he swatted me away.

"It's these invisible banana peels," Stieg explained to his friends. "I keep tripping over them."

"They're a real pain," one of his friends (I can never remember their names) agreed.

"Worse than invisible potholes," the other (Dana, I think) added.

Soon they were all smiling . . . and I was hovering, without a thing to do.

"I gotta go," Stieg told his friends. They said their good-byes. Stieg walked off. I followed.

I let him have his distance for a block or two. Then I caught up.

"Did that happen a lot today?" I asked.

Stieg sighed.

"My hands were shaking so hard in math class that Mrs. Fredrich asked me if I was on drugs," he answered. "Oh, and I'm probably the first person in the history of the middle school to fall into his own locker without being pushed. Luckily, it didn't swing shut. Although the day might have been cooler if I'd stayed inside."

"So the earthquake thing hasn't gone away?" I asked.

Stieg rolled his eyes. "You could say that."

"Do you want to talk about it?"

"Sure. But not with you."

I didn't know what to say to that. I just walked alongside him, wondering whether I could catch him if he fell again. We were passing our elementary school playground. When Stieg was little, he and I would play there all the time. We would slide and tumble around on the jungle gyms. Then our parents died, and Stieg didn't want to play anymore. Not with me, at least.

We continued walking. I sensed something was strange before I realized what it was. The sound of a car engine. Following us. I turned around and saw a black Buick keeping our pace. I gestured to Stieg. He turned around and looked, too. As if this were a signal, the car sped up and pulled ahead of us. Then it braked.

Stieg and I stopped walking.

The car door opened.

Agent Taggart stepped out.

Without another word, Stieg and I started to run.

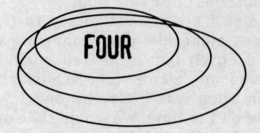

FOUR

We bolted for the playground. There were plenty of people around — kids and parents, doing their after-school kid-and-parent thing.

I turned to see Agent Taggart following us. He was alone.

"I just want to talk!" he yelled.

Stieg got to the jungle gym and started to climb. I followed closely behind. First graders jostled out of our way.

We reached the top rung. Taggart's head was right below our sneakers.

"I want you to listen," he said. The parents eyed him suspiciously, just as I'd hoped they would. Taggart was ignoring them, just as he ignored the children running puppylike around his feet.

"We're listening," I stated flatly. More

than anything, I wanted him to go away. Preferably forever.

"Your grandfather is a smart man," Taggart began. The sun was behind us — he had to shade his eyes. "He's certainly rattled my cage. Had the supervisors come down on me full force. But I want to tell you this: I know about what you call the Sense. I know what you are up to. I want to help. And if you don't let me help, I am going to help anyway. I am going to be watching you. Every breath you take. Every move you make —"

"We know the song," Stieg interrupted. "But you can't touch us."

Taggart smiled. I hated his insincere, sinister smile.

"No, I can't touch you. Not officially. But I want to express to you how easily the situation could change. You have no idea how vulnerable you are. What if your grandfather was found to be incapable of taking care of you? What if he was caught doing something illegal?"

"You're bluffing," I said. But my voice betrayed me. I felt — and sounded — vulnerable. What if he framed Grandfather? What would happen?

Stieg didn't seem to be as bothered.

"Get a job!" he shouted, kicking out at the agent.

"You *are* my job," Taggart chillingly replied.

I thought he would continue. But obviously he thought he had been threatening enough. He stared at us for a long moment, saluted, and walked back to his car.

I turned to Stieg. He had begun to tremble.

"Stieg?" I asked.

"Just quaky, I guess," he whispered. I wasn't so sure.

Maybe he was afraid.

I helped him down. A little girl came over to us and asked if we would be her princes. I told her she could do better. She said "okay" and moved on to the next group of boys.

Stieg and I walked to the street. Taggart's car was still there.

"What do you want to do?" I asked.

Stieg looked at me gravely.

"This is our life now," he said. "We'd better just walk."

So we did.

Agent Taggart followed us all the way home.

He was rarely more than a block away.

Stieg and I didn't talk. We couldn't think of anything to say. The drone of the engine was more conversation than we could take.

The walk home had never seemed so long. I half-expected Taggart to pull into our driveway and come inside with us.

Instead, he kept driving, waving to us before he pulled away. Stieg ran inside the house and called out for Grandfather.

When we told him what had happened, Grandfather was furious. I'd rarely seen him so angry. He immediately called some members of the Network. We kept looking out the window for any sign of Taggart. Even when we moved into the Maze, there were security cameras to keep track of our doorstep visitors.

We were in a bind. We couldn't call the local police if Taggart returned. We couldn't call anyone who didn't already know about the Sense. Because the whole point was to avoid detection. The moment word got out, we'd never be able to live our own lives again. There would always be camera crews and talk-show hosts and scientific inquiries. And the Sense might be disrupted.

We couldn't let that happen.

Gradually our panic subsided. We had more everyday stuff to deal with — even though I was being tracked by a federal agent, I still had to do my homework. When I was done, I offered to help Stieg with his. We were in the Nerve Center. He was playing a video game.

"Not right now," he said, gesturing me to get out of the way.

I went back to my computer and began an E-mail to Rachel and Zach Ede. Then the room went quiet. At first, I didn't notice the change. Then, out of the corner of my eye, I saw that Stieg had turned off his game.

But he was still staring at the TV screen.

The blank TV screen.

"What is it?" I asked. But Stieg wouldn't turn. He was concentrating on the screen. I walked closer. I scanned the TV for some sort of image. But all I could see was the reflection of the room, shaded in gray.

"Can you see it?" Stieg asked.

"No," I whispered.

Stieg nodded.

"It's the earthquake," he said. "I can see it. The rubble — the doll winking at me. Then I can see a woman. I've seen her before. And behind her there's this . . . white carousel horse."

"What does the woman look like?"

Stieg's gaze didn't leave the empty screen. "Short brown hair. She's wearing a white button-down shirt. She's saying something. I don't know what. I know her. I've had this dream before."

He spoke as if hypnotized. He spoke quietly, dictating the contents of a dream. Then he pulled back. His face fell a little, and I could tell the vision was gone. I grabbed a piece of paper and wrote down everything he'd said.

"What just happened?" Stieg turned to me and asked. That's when I knew for sure that he was back.

"I don't know," I admitted. "Do you remember anything?"

"I remember. I just don't understand it. The woman was so familiar, you know? But I can't figure out who she was."

It was the first real clue we had. "Was she someone from around here?" I asked.

Stieg shook his head. "I don't think so."

"How old was she?"

"About Mom and Dad's age. Actually . . ." Stieg's voice trailed off.

"What?"

"It might be a friend of Mom and Dad's. From a while ago. Someone we visited or something."

I listed a few names. People we'd seen recently.

None of them connected. When Grandfather passed by the door and asked what was going on, we explained the problem.

"There's only one thing you can do," Grandfather said thoughtfully. "You should look at the pictures."

Stieg sat up abruptly. "I can't," he protested.

"You have to," I said.

"No I don't," Stieg argued defiantly.

But deep down, he knew he did.

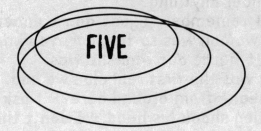

FIVE

The pictures.
Our parents' pictures.
Our dead parents' pictures.
Happy pictures from happy times. Smiles for the camera. Far-off places. Before the storms. After the storms.

I had sorted through the pictures over many sleepless midnights, starting the night after my parents' death, as I sat in my old bed and hoped that somehow my parents could make it home. I had this urgency — I had this fear that I might forget, that I hadn't been paying enough attention while they were alive.

Stieg wouldn't go near the photos. He wouldn't go near anything having to do with our parents. Which was hard, because our parents were everywhere. They were linked in our memory to everything else in our old house, from the books on the shelves to the spoons in the kitchen drawer. Stieg found this unbearable, so when Grandfather whisked us off to his mansion, Stieg didn't protest. He packed his things and moved along in an almost ghostlike trance, as if an essential part of him had died with our parents . . . and could never be brought back to life.

Even two years later, Stieg still didn't talk about our parents. He certainly didn't talk about what had happened to them. Therapists, guidance counselors, distant family members . . . everyone tried to get him to open up. But it didn't work. He refused. He acted as if it was strange for them to bring the subject up. He moved on.

I waited for him to explode. I always felt like *I* was going to explode, that the unfairness and the sadness and the wrongness would all join together and burst from inside of me. I thought Stieg had to be going through the same thing . . . and that sooner or later, he'd give in and let it out.

But no. He never did.

Instead we had moments like these: Stieg and me sitting in front of the photos, with Stieg looking away. Grandfather sitting behind us, obviously concerned.

I didn't tell Stieg he had to look. Instead,

I went through the pictures and pulled out the ones that showed brown-haired women. I passed over hundreds of images of my mother and father — the images that were slowly becoming the heart of my memories, since photos are so much easier to remember than actual events. Every time I paused to look at my parents, Grandfather urged me along. There was no time to waste. The earthquake could happen tomorrow.

Or today.

Eventually, I amassed a large stack of photos to show Stieg.

He was shivering.

"Are you cold?" Grandfather asked.

Stieg shook his head.

"I don't know why I'm shivering," he said. "Let's just get this over with."

I handed him the photos. I looked into his eyes as he thumbed through them. I looked to see if his heart would lurch. I looked to make sure our parents were still registering.

I was still waiting for him to explode.

Or, at the very least, to cry.

But instead, he acted as if he was looking at someone else's family pictures, doing us a favor by looking for a brown-haired stranger.

"Have you found her?" I kept asking, every time Stieg paused. Finally, Grandfather told me to be quiet and let Stieg concentrate.

Ten slow minutes passed. Then Stieg suddenly dealt one of the photos from the stack, as if it were the ace of spades.

"It's her, I think."

I picked up the photo. Stieg was right: She was someone I recognized, but couldn't name. I handed the image to Grandfather.

He began to laugh.

"Oh my!" he said. "Oh my, indeed."

"Who is it?"

"It's Piper Hoffman. A friend of your mother's."

"Where is she?"

Grandfather thought for a moment. The smile fell from his face. His voice turned grave.

"She lives right outside of San Francisco," he said quietly.

At first, I didn't understand his tone. Then I realized:

San Francisco.

An earthquake in San Francisco.

It was going to happen again.

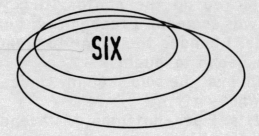

SIX

"It wasn't the Big One," my father wrote in 1989, "but it was close."

An earthquake measuring 7.1 on the Richter scale had just hit San Francisco and its surrounding towns. My parents were in Candlestick Park when it happened, watching the World Series. (The Sense had led them there.) They felt the ground shake the stadium. They rushed out in the flow of chaos that ensued. Luckily, casualties for the quake, known as the Loma Prieta earthquake, were minimal. But damage was high. A wake-up call had rung. The city was still vulnerable.

It is easy to understand why San Francisco lives in fear of The Big One. The quake of 1906 devastated the city. Few buildings were left standing. Everybody's lives were affected — mostly for the worse.

In the days that followed that quake, my great-grandfather roamed the city, helping to fight fires and look for survivors. If there's one thing that I've learned from the Chronicles, it's that fire is an earthquake's deadly accomplice; as gas lines and furnaces crumble, a firestorm is unleashed. In San Francisco, in both 1906 and 1989, fire caused more damage than the actual shifting of the earth.

This is what my great-grandfather wrote in an entry dated April 21, 1906:

ASHES and RUBBLE. The whole city is ASHES and RUBBLE. I do not know where to begin. The night is lit red by the fires. Everyone looks as if they had crawled through HELL to remain here. The death and destruction are HORRIFIC. Even I, who have seen other such tragedies, am utterly dazed by it all.

Where can I begin? The City Emergency Hospital caved in during that fateful minute, burying nurses, doctors, and patients in a mass of ASHES and RUBBLE. We are desperate for medical supplies. The sick and injured are spread on street corners, awaiting help.

The Valencia Hotel, formerly four

stories high, is now a mere one story above the ground. Many dead are trapped inside. The Palace Hotel survived the tremblor, only to be pierced by flames. We all thought it could withstand damage. We looked to its flag as a sign of hope. Then it was lost in a rush of smoke and flames. The opera singer Enrico Caruso was in the hotel and fled quickly. I have heard that after the first tremor was over, he ran to his window and sang an aria, just to make sure his voice was intact. Numerous people I have met said they heard this unbeliev-able song as they fled from their homes. It added to the feeling of complete absurdity.

The firemen are exhausted. The build-ing that houses the alarm system has been destroyed. Water is extremely scarce. I have heard that there are underground storage tanks of water, which are now out of reach — the pipes have broken, and there is no way of retrieving the water.

In order to stop the fires, they have used DYNAMITE to destroy build-ings in the flames' path, with the hope of preventing the fire from spreading through them. (If the fire is not fed by the buildings . . . if there is only empty space . . . it will die out. Or so we hope.) We ran into each building beforehand to search for survivors. I found an old woman in her bed, too scared to move. She screamed when I lifted her, even though I explained to her that the building was about to be destroyed. I don't think she was screaming at me. I think she was screaming at FATE.

Roadways have SPLIT OPEN. Buildings sit at BIZARRE angles, always on the verge of collapse. Trees have FALLEN and TWISTED — some are unrecognizable as trees. Gravestones lie like broken dominoes. Statues are toppled and beheaded. Dead horses line the streets.

The Mint and the Post Office still stand, but they are surrounded by devastation. The Opera House: in ashes. St. Patrick's Church: burned to the ground, its steeple collapsed into the street. The Examiner building: gone. And then the Palace Hotel. Destroyed.

The buildings are still burning.

Everything around us is SMOLDERING — especially the ashes in our hearts. What I want now, more than anything else, is rest. But that will not come.

There is so much to do. After such horror, there is always so much to do.

My grandfather stayed in San Francisco for more than a month, helping to rebuild.

All in all, 497 city blocks were destroyed in the quakes and fires of 1906, covering 2,831 acres. 28,000 buildings were destroyed. Mansions. City Hall. Apartments. Offices. Theaters. Schools.

Everything.

All of the city records were burned and destroyed. Over 250,000 people — more than half the city's population — were left homeless.

More than a thousand people had been injured.

Seven hundred had died.

The city's past and present were destroyed. It could only look to the future. It rebuilt.

But always, *always*, there is the fear of the next earthquake.

The Big One.

Was this what Stieg and I were headed for?

Were we retracing our great-grandfather's steps?

   Only this time, it would be worse.
   Much worse.
   I was afraid.

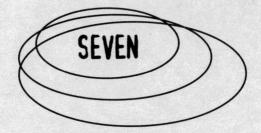

SEVEN

We had to find Piper Hoffman.

Quickly.

We ransacked all of our available resources. My parents' old letters. The San Francisco white pages. The Internet.

All we could find was a slip of paper, folded into my mother's final address book:

PH 1001 1/2 Castro.

It was all we had to go on. As we sat in the airplane, headed toward San Francisco, I kept the piece of paper in my palm, as if it could act as some sort of homing device. I knew we were getting closer. I didn't know what we'd find.

There hadn't been a listing for Piper Hoffman in any of the directories. Not at 1001 1/2 Castro Street. Not anywhere.

I had looked for references to Piper Hoffman in the Chronicles, but couldn't find any. This made sense, if Piper was just a friend; the Chronicles are a record of my parents' second life, the life of the Sense. Their first life hardly earns a mention.

Grandfather reinforced this belief. He said Piper wasn't someone whom my parents had saved. Instead, she was a childhood friend of my mother's. Grandfather struggled to remember what she did now for a living — he thought she was some sort of scientist, but he wasn't sure.

I asked him if Piper Hoffman knew about the Sense.

He didn't know. He hadn't kept track of my mother's friendships. He couldn't even remember if Piper had come to the funeral. He thought so. But it had all passed in such a rush . . . once again, he wasn't sure.

We didn't have time for him to think any further. We quickly made plans and fabricated excuses. We had to get to San Francisco.

Stieg resisted. He knew he had to go. And at the same time, he didn't want to go. He wanted to stay home. He wanted to stay in school. He wanted to be with his friends.

He hated the Sense. He screamed this to me as I packed his things.

I was calm. I was insistent. I zipped his bag emphatically.

He opened the bag while I wasn't looking.

He started to unpack his things. I blocked him. He continued to pull things from the bag, not even bothering to put them back in their drawers. Just throwing them.

I told him to stop. I tried to gather his clothes.

He shoved me away.

I shoved him back.

He glared.

At that moment, I could see that he hated me as much as he hated the Sense.

I stood firm.

He decided. He could have yelled further. But he gave in. He left the room.

As soon as he was out the door, I started shaking. I didn't want it to be this way.

I thought about our parents. Sometimes they hadn't wanted to go. Sometimes my mother had to stay while my father — the one with the Sense — had to leave. She asked him not to. She begged him not to.

He missed seeing my first-grade play. I was Narrator #1. I didn't care that he was doing "something important" (which is how it had been explained to me). I wanted him to see me in my suit, reading my three lines. I wanted him to be there. So many times, I had wanted my parents to be there. But they couldn't. There was always the Sense.

This is what I thought about as I repacked Stieg's things, picking them up from where he'd thrown them. I thought about the times my parents had been taken away from us. I thought about all of the time that was yet to come, all the things they wouldn't see.

I realized that I could hate the Sense, too.

Not enough to want it gone. Not enough to erase all of the lives that had been saved, and all of the lives that had yet to be saved.

But almost.

After I'd packed Stieg's bag, I found him in our backyard. It was late, and the stars were just beginning to emerge from the night.

Stieg wouldn't look at me. He just looked up.

"Are you ready?" I asked.

"Do I have a choice?" he replied.

I shook my head.

"Well, that's your answer, then," he murmured. That was the worst part for him — he didn't have any choice.

He walked back into the house without waiting for me. By the time I had followed, he had moved our suitcases out into the hall. He chatted with Grandfather as if nothing had happened.

As if this was all perfectly normal.

When we left the house, we looked for Taggart's car. There wasn't any sign of him.

Which didn't mean he wasn't there.

Dr. Nisson picked us up and drove us to the airport. A member of the Network who worked for an airline had arranged our tickets, under assumed names. No questions asked.

I checked my wallet and made sure I had my ATM card. Our parents had left Stieg and me a large inheritance, with no strings attached. We were lucky enough to be able to go wherever we wanted, whenever we needed to.

By the time we got onto the plane, it was hard for me to believe that just a few hours earlier, we had been in school. We had been given a brief glimpse of our first life.

And then our second life resumed.

We took a cab from the airport. Morning had just begun. We headed straight for Castro Street — hoping desperately that we'd find Piper Hoffman there.

The buildings grew closer to one another as we neared the city. The city that had been destroyed in 1906 was a shining city once more. It had rebuilt quickly. Within days of the quake, aid had come pouring in.

What would happen if a quake struck again? Yes, buildings are stronger now. But the ground would still rise and fall. People would still die.

They had died in 1906. They had died in 1800, 1857, 1885, 1961, and 1989 as well.

There was no escape from this fact.

Topographically, San Francisco is unlike any other city in the world. Castro Street, like many San Francisco streets, is a series of ups and downs — hills and valleys of exasperating steepness. Riding in our cab was like being in a four-door roller coaster. There was no such thing as even ground.

Suddenly, the ride stopped, halfway up a hill.

"One-thousand-one-and-a-half Castro," the cabbie announced. I could only see 1001, but figured 1001 1/2 couldn't be too far away.

Stieg and I hadn't spoken much during the trip — only instructions and bare politenesses. ("Turn here." "Close the window." "Do you have any gum?") Now that we were at Castro Street, I tried to jostle him into wakefulness.

"We're here," I announced, shouldering our bags to the corner.

"Duh, Adam."

"Are you ready?" I asked.

"Ready as I'll never be."

There was a small path at the side of 1001 Castro Street. As I'd expected, it led to a small door, over which hung a sign for 1001 1/2.

Bingo.

I went to press the doorbell. Sure, it was still early in the morning. But there wasn't a moment to lose.

I rang the bell. Then I looked at the little nameplate on the door.

Jen, Tinka, and Terry.

No Piper.

This was not good.

Stieg smirked when he saw this. I was telling him to be serious when the door opened.

It wasn't Piper Hoffman, unless Piper Hoffman had transformed herself into a short-haired twenty-four-year-old.

It was Jen, Tinka, or Terry, keeping the chain on the door and wondering why she had two kids with suitcases on her doorstep.

Oops.

"Can I help you?" Jen-Tinka-Terry asked.

"We're looking for Piper Hoffman," I explained.

"Who?"

"Piper Hoffman."

"I think you have the wrong house."

I asked if this was, in fact, 1001 1/2 Castro Street.

"The one and only," the woman replied.

"You see, a friend of our mother's lives here. Or, I guess, used to live here. And we thought she was here . . ." I blathered, trying to prolong the period before she closed the door on me.

"Who is it, Jen?" a voice behind the door asked. Soon, another woman — with short blonde hair and piercing eyes — peered around the doorway.

"You know them?" Jen asked.

"Should I?"

"Do you know Piper Hoffman?" I interjected.

"No. Should I?"

"Piper Hoffman?" a third voice — a male voice — asked.

The two women turned inside and nodded.

"Don't know her," the man responded.

Jen shot me an impatient glance.

"One second," she said. Then she closed the door.

I could hear the voices on the other side: "They're obviously looking for a former tenant." "They don't look dangerous." "I'm sure I've never heard of Piper Kaufman." "Maybe she's the one who left the kitchen chairs. . . ."

I shuffled from foot to foot. Stieg sighed and sat down on one of our suitcases.

The door reopened.

Jen was smiling this time.

"Come in," she said, beckoning us through the door.

We walked right into the living room. Every

tabletop and desk space seemed to be covered with pink streamers, silver balloons, and Barbie party goods — napkins, cardboard tiaras, the works.

"We had a Barbie-Q this weekend," Jen explained. Then she introduced herself, Tinka (the other woman), and Terry (the man).

"We were just headed to work," Tinka said, pulling a notebook from under a Barbie party hat.

"Where's my backpack?" Terry asked. He shot a look in our direction. "Is he okay?"

I didn't know what he meant. Then I followed his glance to Stieg, who had begun to shake. Jen, Tinka, and Terry immediately cleared off their lime-green couch and helped me guide Stieg off his feet.

"What's going on?" Jen asked.

"It's okay," I said feebly.

"Does he need medicine?" Tinka chimed in, holding Stieg's hand as he continued to quake.

"No, it will be fine in a second." And sure enough, the tremors calmed down almost as soon as they'd started. Stieg mumbled an apology.

"Don't be silly," Terry told him. "Nobody apologizes in this house without a good reason."

Stieg smiled wanly and I explained once more who we were looking for. Jen walked to a filing cabinet and took out a folder marked *Apartment,* but she couldn't find any mention of a previous tenant.

"You could ask Mrs. Amata," Tinka suggested.

"That's a great idea," Jen agreed.

"Mrs. Amata lives upstairs," Terry explained. "She's been here since the Gold Rush."

"Is she awake?" I asked.

Terry, Jen, and Tinka all shared a laughing look. Then Jen let me in on the joke.

"Mrs. Amata is *always* awake," she told me. "In the middle of the night, you can hear her walking and talking. Yelling, arguing, pacing."

"Who's she talking to?" Stieg asked.

"The spirits," Terry replied. "Mrs. Amata likes to talk to the spirits."

"Let's go," Jen said, knocking aside a Barbie plate to reach her keys. "She's probably waiting for us."

"Can you walk?" Tinka asked Stieg. He nodded and stood up.

"WE'RE COMING!" Terry yelled to the ceiling.

In response, I swear I heard a laugh.

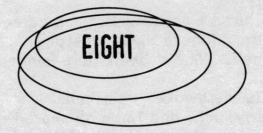

EIGHT

All five of us walked to the front of the house and rang the bell. The door buzzed open without a word from upstairs.

"She's up there. Good luck," Terry said, pointing to a dimly lit stairway.

"Aren't you coming?" Tinka asked him as she opened the door.

"I can't be late for work," Terry shrugged.

"Me, neither, I'm afraid," Jen added.

Tinka sighed. "Well, we can't just leave them alone."

"I don't think she eats kids on the first date," Terry assured her.

"Oh, go ahead," Tinka said after a moment's thought. "I'll stay here. I can be late today."

Terry and Jen wished us well. When the

door closed behind us, the house was dark as night.

Cautiously, Tinka started up the stairway. Stieg and I followed.

"Hello?" I called. Tinka put out a hand to stop me. I didn't know why, but we had to walk in silence. Only it wasn't really silence. There was the creaking of the steps under our feet. The whir of faraway cars. The clinking of the bracelets Tinka wore on her wrist.

And the laugh . . . quiet first, then a little louder.

We walked toward it.

"This way," Tinka whispered from the top of the stairs, pointing to a door around the corner.

"This way," an older voice echoed.

Tinka opened the door and peered around the doorway. Then she gestured for us to come in.

The room was lit by candles, suffocating the air with the smell and heat of melting wax. The windows were covered with grim tapestries. The furniture was dark wood. It was a room that was destined to be dusty. And yet, the tabletops shone clean.

"Mrs. Amata?" Tinka asked. At first, I didn't know who she was talking to. Then I saw the woman in the chair. Her legs, wrapped in an afghan, didn't touch the floor. Her face was turned away from us — looking at the window, as if it wasn't covered. As if she could see right through.

"I've brought these two boys —" Tinka began to explain.

Mrs. Amata cut her off.

"I *know* who you've brought," she said impatiently. Her voice was an echo of a rasp. I leaned forward to hear what she said.

"Come closer," she spoke, turning now to greet our glances. In the flicker of the candlelight, I could see her face — alabaster white, crowned with eerie raven-black hair. She smiled gently. Stieg and I stepped forward. Tinka, as if she'd been told to do so, stayed behind.

"So you've come to talk about the earthquake?" Mrs. Amata asked.

"Actually, they're looking for a woman named —" Tinka began.

"Silence!" Mrs. Amata ordered. "I know why they are here." She turned from Tinka to Stieg. "They want to know about the earthquake. I was a young girl then. One of the survivors."

Tinka sighed. I could imagine she'd heard this story before. She thought Mrs. Amata was about to ride off on a tangent. But I was willing to listen, if only for a short while. Somehow I knew Mrs. Amata would get back to the present.

"Everyone's forgotten now," Mrs. Amata continued. "But I can never forget. My father was a banker. A very respectable man, always early to rise and early to work. The day of the quake was no exception. My mother, my sister Allegra, and I were all sleeping when the first quake hit. It woke us up, sure enough. Flung us out of bed — Allegra was crying before she hit the ground.

"None of us knew what was happening. We ran for Mother, but the house began to tilt. The second quake came and knocked us to the ground again. The house fell with us. We were crying 'Mama' and 'Papa' but it was no use.

"Allegra and I held each other's hands. Everything fell apart, right on top of us. Wood and brick and porcelain and curtain fabric — it all tumbled together, and we fell with it. We were buried alive. I couldn't see Allegra, but I could hear her voice and, after a few minutes, we managed to reach each other with our hands. Even when our voices were hoarse from screaming, we would squeeze each other's hands, just to make sure we were both still alive.

"An hour passed. It seemed like much longer. A man heard our voices. He called over to our mother — who had gotten out okay — and the two of them dug until their hands bled. We weren't too far down. Soon other people helped, and the debris above us was removed. When the daylight came through, it was glorious. The man pulled me out. A stranger. Then Allegra was freed. We were both okay — only bruises. We were lucky.

"The man never told us his name. He disappeared as soon as he saw we were all right. Mother ran to find Father at the bank. When she arrived, they were pulling safes and furniture out of the building. The fires had started and the flames were getting closer by the second. Within minutes, the whole block was aflame. The safes stayed in the middle of the street. We couldn't open them for weeks. They were too hot. If we had opened them, the air would have vaporized all the money inside."

Mrs. Amata paused for a second. I wondered about the man who had saved her. I wondered if it could have been my great-grandfather. It could just as easily have been one of the hundreds of other heroes from the quake. But still . . . I wished I had a photo of Christopher Atwood, to show Mrs. Amata. I had very little doubt that she would recognize him . . . *if* he had been the one.

I glanced at my companions. Tinka was looking at her watch and Stieg was itching to sit down. But the old woman waved away their impatience. After another short breath, she continued.

"I lost my cat. Sometimes I still think I see her out of the corner of my eye. Allegra was never the same again. She startled when a car passed by, thinking it was another quake. She died a nervous woman, I'm sorry to say. I was made of stronger stuff. You don't get to be my age without strength."

"Mrs. Amata —" Tinka said gently.

The older woman held up her hand again. "I know, I know. This isn't why you're here. And at the same time, it is. Am I right?"

I nodded.

"Good. Now who are you looking for?"

"Piper Hoffman. She used to live downstairs."

"Piper Hoffman . . . oh, that must have been some time ago."

"Please try to remember," I said. "It's important."

"I *know* it's important," Mrs. Amata snapped. "People don't come up here unless it's important. Yes, Piper Hoffman. A beautiful name. A lovely girl. Not that long ago, after all. Maybe three years. We talked a lot about the earthquakes. She was one of those earthquake doctors — what are they called?"

"Seismologists?" I offered.

Mrs. Amata nodded emphatically. "Yes, that's it. Of course."

"Do you know where she is now?" Stieg asked.

Mrs. Amata lifted herself from her chair. It was not a quick process. Tinka moved in to help, but Mrs. Amata huffed her away.

Slowly, Mrs. Amata shuffled (with the aid of a cane) to a desk on the other side of the room. The desktop was immaculately organized; it only took a moment for her to find what she was looking for. From what I could see, it was an ancient-looking address book — a telephone book from the era before telephones. She flipped the pages until she found the right name. Then she wrote something down on a piece of paper.

My hopes lifted.

Closing the address book, Mrs. Amata stood up straight and walked over to me.

"Here it is," she said, handing me the piece of paper, folded in half.

I thanked her.

"My pleasure," she said, easing herself back to her chair. It took her nearly as long to sit down as it did to stand up.

"Well, I guess we'll be going," Tinka announced. I hoped she wasn't too late for work.

"Good-bye then," Mrs. Amata murmured.

I was going to thank her again, but her expression stopped me. She was listening to someone. But nobody was speaking.

Tinka led us to the door. After she'd left, Mrs. Amata spoke again. Stieg and I stepped back to hear.

"You know what's going to happen, don't you?" she said. From where we stood, she was shadowed within the chair.

"Yes," Stieg answered.

"You have a way of knowing," Mrs. Amata continued.

"Yes," Stieg said again.

"Do what you can. Do all that you can." Mrs. Amata sighed. Then she turned inward again, silent. Stieg and I held on for a moment more. But she'd said what she wanted to say.

We moved on.

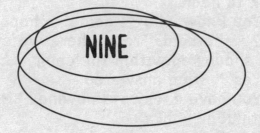

NINE

The phone was ringing when we got back to Tinka's apartment. She ran to answer it. We waited in the Barbie-Q'ed living room.

"Oh, hi," she said, her voice lowering to a raspy moan. "Yes. . . . No, I wasn't over-sleeping. I'm afraid I have the thing that's going around. . . . Yeah, the flu. Or maybe it's something viral. . . . Oh, no — I'll come right in. I mean, I doubt it's contagious. . . . Yes, it could be what Mary had." At this point, Tinka winked at us and held the phone away from her ear. I could hear the man on the other end arguing his point. After a minute of this, Tinka pulled the receiver back to her ear. "Yes . . . I guess you're right. I'll stay home."

Hanging up the phone, she turned to us and sighed.

"There are advantages to having a boss who's afraid of germs," she explained. "But enough of that. Where are we going?"

"I don't know if you want to come along," I said seriously.

"Why don't you read the address before you say that?" Stieg asked, pointing to the slip of paper in my hand. Smiling at Tinka, he added, "We might need a car."

She smiled back and nodded.

"Do you want me to leave you two alone?" I asked.

Their smiles quick-changed into annoyance. I opened the paper. In Mrs. Amata's ancient, curlicued handwriting, it read:

Piper Hoffman 4 Randall's Peak. San Flora, California No phone

"No phone?" Stieg read aloud. We tried directory assistance. The number was unlisted.

"Well, we'll just have to make a surprise visit," Tinka concluded.

I asked her why she was helping us.

She shrugged. "Because Mrs. Amata wanted me to. *That* was clear. And Mrs. Amata never wants to help anybody. So you two must really be worth helping. Anyway, San Flora is over two hours away. That would be a supremely expensive cab ride."

"We have the money," I huffed.

"Well, save your money and buy me dinner afterward, okay?"

63

"Do you know how to get there?"

"Sure I know how to get there. Randall's Peak is right by the amusement park."

"The amusement park?" Stieg gasped. I didn't get it at first. Then I remembered.

The carousel.

"Yeah, there's a pretty cool amusement park nearby," Tinka continued, not noticing Stieg's reaction. "We could go there if your friend isn't home."

We were in the car in a matter of minutes (it took a little while for Tinka to find her keys). She drove a convertible Volkswagen — very vintage, very cool. With our bags in the backseat beside Stieg, we headed out of the city.

As we traveled north, I thought once more about the Great Quake of 1906. San Francisco hadn't been the only city hit. The whole area fell to its knees during the initial tremor. To the north of the city, bridges snapped and huge redwoods fell like sticks. A quicksilver mine collapsed, killing the miners. A two-story hotel fell into Tomales Bay. The earth became a minefield of fires and chasms.

No one was safe.

Stieg loved Tinka's convertible, waving his arms in the air, enjoying the ride despite his deeper fears. I couldn't enjoy it.

I wanted to reach Piper Hoffman.

I wanted to see if she knew what to do. It heartened me to learn that she was a seismologist. Maybe that's why the Sense was sending us to her.

Tinka blasted the radio. The tunes were infectious. But the closer we got, the more somber Stieg became. I watched him in the rearview mirror. He put his hands down. He began to stare at the pavement.

"No," I heard him say. I turned to him and his stare matched mine, word for word. His fingers were now digging into the seat. Clawing. Trying to hold on. He wasn't shaking, but I could tell the earthquake was there. It was inside of him. It was tearing him apart.

I wanted to stop the car. I wanted to climb into the backseat and tell Stieg that everything would be okay. But neither action would help. We had to choose speed over caution. We had to choose truth over lies.

How deep could the Sense go? The Chronicles held many warnings. My father, my grandfather, my great-grandfather — every one of the Sense's possessors had felt it wrestle within his core. It formed a pain that would not stop. It became a thought that would not go away. Every one of the Atwoods had warned: The Sense can destroy a person.

Like the disasters it foretells, the Sense erupts. It avalanches. It quakes.

Stieg held on. He closed his eyes. I leaned over the back of my seat and told him to think of blueberry pancakes and Scooby Doo and clean white tablecloths. Anything but earthquakes. Grandfather's eyes. The full moon. A winning soccer game.

"I keep seeing her," he said, all happiness drained from his voice. "She's chasing after the carousel horse. The world is falling apart. I can't get there."

"We're closer," I assured him. "We're getting closer."

"But we won't be there. I keep seeing it. Everyone is dying."

Tinka turned down the radio. With the song now wavering in the background, she shot us a long, hard look.

"Is he okay?" she asked.

"I'm fine," Stieg replied. But his voice sounded frail.

"Should we go to a doctor?"

"We know how to handle it," I assured her. "It's a family condition."

"Are you sure there's nothing we can do?"

Of course I wasn't sure.

"I'm absolutely sure," I said automatically. What could Tinka do?

We drove on, passing vineyards and wineries. Stieg unclenched, but couldn't relax.

Tinka tried conversation, but it fell lifeless into the space between her concerns and our own.

The songs on the radio shifted into the news. I listened closely, waiting for the word *earthquake* to be said. As if there would be a warning. (There are hardly ever any earthquake warnings.) As if, somehow, someone else would know.

But no one else would know. We were the last of the Atwoods. And the other family with a warning similar to the Sense — the Edes — was nowhere in sight.

I watched Tinka concentrate on the road as she drove. I didn't know what to say to her. Should I warn her? Would she think we were crazy? Would we be risking our privacy?

But what if we could help? What if a few well-timed words could save Tinka's life?

I waited until Tinka said it would just be a few more minutes until San Flora. Signs for the Wonder World Amusement Park were popping up every half-mile.

"Don't you wonder why we're in such a hurry?" I asked. In the rearview mirror, I could see Stieg take notice.

"Of course I wonder," Tinka said, still looking at the road. "But I figured by now that you wouldn't tell me. And I'm not the kind of girl who'll pry."

"If I tell you, will you take me seriously?"

"How old are you?"

"Fourteen."

"I'll tell you what — I promise to take you seriously. And I haven't taken a fourteen-year-old seriously since I turned ten."

"There's going to be an earthquake," I said bluntly. "That's why we're in a hurry. We know there's going to be an earthquake."

"Do you want me to drive faster?" Tinka asked. I couldn't tell if she was joking.

"I'm serious," I said.

"Oh, I'm serious, too. Do you want me to drive faster?"

"As fast as you can without getting us in trouble."

Tinka hit the accelerator and the engine vroomed. The wind blew faster. I could barely hear the radio, or Tinka.

"When is it going to be?" she shouted.

"We don't know."

She nodded and drove on. Soon, a Ferris wheel peeked over the horizon. A roller coaster. A free-fall ride.

A carousel.

I couldn't see it. But somehow, at seventy-five miles an hour, with wind in my ears, I could hear its singsong chimes. Like a music box, amplified.

I looked in the rearview mirror. Stieg had frozen in place.

He heard it, too.

I yelled to Tinka, asking her if she heard it.

But by the time I had finished my question, the sound was gone.

Stieg could still hear it.

"Turn right," he said.

"It's not this exit," Tinka argued.

"Turn right. Now!"

Tinka put on her blinker and swerved into the right-lane exit. The ramp looped us around dizzily. Tinka took this in stride, following the signs to Wonder World. Soon we were edging along its fence, hearing the accumulated voices of hundreds of parkgoers. Screams from the roller coaster. Chatter as bright as the colored balloons that hung from the fence. The whoosh and roar of the free fall.

"Do you want me to stop?" Tinka asked.

I shook my head.

We had to get to Piper Hoffman.

It didn't take us long. The street narrowed. The hills intervened. Although the amusement park could still be heard in the background, it fell out of sight. Instead, trees regained their ground. Houses were fewer and far between. Traffic grew scarce.

"Randall's Peak," Tinka announced as we turned onto a rugged, twisting road. We looked for number four. Which shouldn't have been hard, since there were only a dozen houses before we hit a dead end.

But there wasn't a number four.

"Her house doesn't exist?" Stieg asked, a strong note of despair in his voice.

"It must be here somewhere." Tinka sighed. We drove back and forth between number two and number twelve for twenty minutes.

Then Stieg saw the path.

It couldn't have been more than three feet wide. No number. Just a white stone at each side.

"That must be it," Stieg said.

"There's no way my car can fit in there," Tinka observed.

"We'll walk," I volunteered. Tinka pulled over — there was just enough space in front of the path to allow a car to pull in from the street.

I began to thank Tinka for the ride, but she interrupted.

"If you think I'm leaving you two alone here, you're crazy," she said, grabbing Stieg's bag. She was the first one out of the car.

I, however, was the first one to the path. There are very few times in my life when I've wished I had a machete. But this was definitely one of them. The path wasn't really a path at all — it was merely a trail of dirt guiding the way, with branches and leaves that viciously interrupted any sense of movement. Since I didn't have anything that could hack away all of the undergrowth, I had to push right through, always looking at the path on the ground. For I knew: If I drifted off the trail, it would be very hard to find it again.

I waded through the bushes and trees, with Tinka's and Stieg's steady sounds behind me. Then there was a light ahead. A clearing. I pushed my way through and found myself in a yard, facing a cabin. It all happened so quickly that I stumbled and nearly fell. Tinka, close on my heels, tripped over me, and Stieg tripped over *her*.

Tinka looked back at where we had come from.

"What was *that*?" she exclaimed, brushing herself off.

"Nature's way of saying *get lost*," I answered, studying the cabin ahead of us. Although it didn't have a sign, I was sure this was the place. I only had to hope that Mrs. Amata's information was up-to-date, and that Piper Hoffman still lived here.

"Listen," Stieg whispered. Suddenly, I heard it. The amusement park, off in the distance. Faint, but present.

"Is anybody home?" Tinka called loudly.

No reply.

We walked closer to the house. A cat crossed my path — calico. I stooped down to pet it.

Then I heard the unmistakable sound of a gun being cocked.

And a voice telling me not to move.

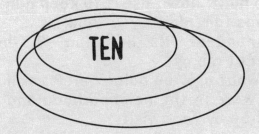

TEN

I kept my eye on the cat. I sensed Stieg and Tinka frozen at my side.

"Who are you?" the voice asked. A woman's voice.

"Adam Atwood. We're Jonathan and Laura Atwood's children."

"Laura didn't have a daughter."

"Tinka drove us here," I explained.

"Okay, then. You can turn around."

If I'd had any doubts, one look at the woman confirmed that it was Piper Hoffman. She looked exactly as she had in my mother's photos. Her hair had a few gray streaks now, and the lines on her face were a little more defined. But other than that, she was absolutely the same. My mother's friend. The woman in Stieg's visions.

I eyed the gun in her hand, which was

now pointed at the ground. She followed my glance.

"Don't worry," she said. "It hasn't been loaded in years. It was my father's. He used it to hunt. Now I use it to keep hunters away. Seems fair, don't you think?"

I nodded. "Ms. Hoffman —" I began. But she cut me off.

"What are you doing here? I fail to believe you were in the neighborhood and happened to drop by for a visit."

I could usually rely on Stieg for a witty comeback. But Stieg was speechless. He kept staring at Piper Hoffman. She noticed this.

"Stop looking and start explaining," she said, impatient. I opened my mouth, but she told me to be quiet. She wanted to hear it from Stieg.

"It's about the qu-qu-quake," he stuttered.

"What quake?"

"The one that's c-c-c-coming."

"I see," Piper Hoffman said. I couldn't tell whether she saw at all.

"They've traveled a long way," Tinka added.

"They've still got a long way to go."

Without another word, my mother's friend walked right past us, sweeping the calico cat up into her arms and heading toward the cabin. In the doorway, she turned and told us to come inside.

She put the rifle into an umbrella rack and ushered us into a small living room. The cabin was bigger than it seemed from the outside, and there were at least three more cats roaming from room to room. The living room was filled with scientific instruments enclosed in glass and metal.

"Broken seismographs," our host explained. "Some of them are antiques. I fix them."

"Mrs. Amata told us you were a seismologist," Tinka said.

"Mrs. Amata? Is *that* how you found me? She must be older than Yoda by now."

I touched one of the glass cases and looked at the white scroll, which kept track of the heartbeat of the earth. Only now it was stopped . . . even though the ground was far from still.

Piper Hoffman was watching us. Since we hadn't been asked to sit, we stood and loitered. Tinka seemed particularly uncomfortable. I felt sorry for bringing her here.

Finally, our host offered us something to drink. When Stieg said, "Thanks, Ms. Hoffman," she told us that it was actually *Doctor* Hoffman. She also said we could sit down.

I took this as a good sign.

I could hear her in the kitchen, opening

the refrigerator, getting out glasses. I thumbed the strap of my bag and looked around the living room for pictures. There was only one: Dr. Hoffman and my mother, photographed a long time ago. Although it was not identical to the picture we'd seen the night before, it looked as if it had been taken from the same roll.

Dr. Hoffman paused in the doorway, three glasses of lemonade in her hands. She saw me holding the photograph.

"I loved your mother very much," she said. "We were almost like sisters. No one could separate us, until she married your father. I think about her every day."

I didn't know what to say to that. Dr. Hoffman continued.

"It's strange to me that you're here. Strange because somehow I expected it."

She didn't explain any further. She passed out our drinks and asked Tinka where she was from, and asked me how Grandfather was. She didn't ask Stieg any questions. But she kept looking at him. I could tell she wanted to ask him something. But she didn't say a word.

Even though we had told her why we had come, none of us spoke about earthquakes. It seemed like an ordinary visit, even though it wasn't ordinary at all.

In a subtle yet unmistakable way, Dr. Hoffman began hinting that Tinka should leave. Asking her how far she had to drive. Thanking her for bringing us here. At first, I didn't understand why she was doing this. Then the realization came to me: Dr. Hoffman knew about the Sense. And she didn't want to talk about it in front of a stranger. She knew why we'd come. But she also knew something of the secrecy involved.

Tinka didn't know what to do. From the glances she stole at her watch, I could tell she was worried about getting home. But I could also tell that she didn't want to leave Stieg and me until she was sure we were safe. The opportunity to reassure her came when Dr. Hoffman left the room to get some tea for herself.

While she was gone, I leaned over to Tinka and told her it was okay if she wanted to leave.

"Are you sure?" she asked.

I told her I was.

She gave us her phone number and said to call at any time if we needed help.

When Dr. Hoffman returned to the living room, Tinka stood and said her good-byes. I was afraid she had forgotten about the warning I'd given her in the car. But she mentioned it on the way out.

"I'll remember what you told me," she said, hugging Stieg and me good-bye. "I'll be careful."

I hoped she would be.

I hoped we had helped.

But there was no way to be sure. Not until the quake had come and gone.

Only then would I know if we'd saved her life.

Dr. Hoffman closed the door behind Tinka. Then she returned to the living room and watched us for a silent moment.

"You told her why you were here?" she asked.

"Sort of."

"Are you going to tell me?"

First I wanted to know how much she already knew.

"Well," she said, sitting down across from me, "I assume this has to do with your father's Sense. Your mother told me about it. She would call me when he was away. Sometimes she was so upset — she had to tell me. She also told me about Stieg. So I imagine that's why you're here."

"I saw you," Stieg whispered. "I saw you on the carousel."

Dr. Hoffman laughed. "The carousel? I haven't been on a carousel in years."

This didn't matter to Stieg.

"I saw you on the carousel," he insisted,

78

his voice stronger now. "During the earthquake."

"What earthquake?"

"The one that hasn't happened yet."

Dr. Hoffman paused for a moment. "How much do you know about me?" she asked.

"Not much," I admitted.

"Did you know that I spend most of my days studying earthquakes? I monitor tremors for the U.S. Earthquake Control Center. There's a real seismograph in the back of this house, in a secure vault. I have spent a large part of my life studying geology and seismology. So please don't be offended if I say that I find it hard to believe that you can waltz right in and tell me when an earthquake is going to occur."

"But you know about our father's Sense," I began.

"Yes. I know about it. But that doesn't mean I believe in it. I honestly don't know what I believe."

"Believe *me*," Stieg said, his voice trembling.

Dr. Hoffman sighed. "Do you know when this earthquake is going to hit?"

"Soon."

"Where?"

"Here. I think."

"Do you understand what this means?"

Stieg shook his head.

"San Flora is near the top of the San Andreas Fault. Do you know what a fault is?"

I knew. But Stieg didn't.

Dr. Hoffman raised an eyebrow at this. "You mean to tell me that you have no idea what causes an earthquake?"

"Not really," Stieg mumbled.

"All right," Dr. Hoffman said, standing up. She left the room for a few minutes and returned with a stack of papers. Placing them atop one of the seismograph cases, she began to tell Stieg about the heart of a quake.

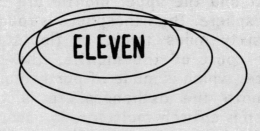

ELEVEN

"To understand earthquakes," Dr. Hoffman began, "you first have to understand the form of the earth."

She passed a diagram over to Stieg, illustrating the different layers of the earth.

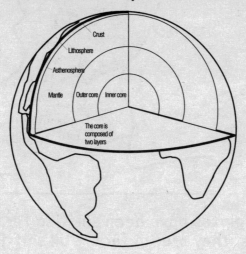

Crust

Lithosphere

Asthenosphere

Mantle   Outer core Inner core

The core is
composed of
two layers

"We live up here, on the crust. It's made of solid rock, from four to forty-five miles thick. Beneath the crust is another layer of solid rock, the upper mantle. Together, the crust and the upper mantle are called the lithosphere. The lithosphere is roughly thirty to sixty miles thick. It floats atop another part of the mantle, the asthenosphere, which is made of partly molten rock. Beneath the asthenosphere is the core, which is entirely molten.

"Although the lithosphere seems solid enough to us, it is actually made up of several tectonic plates. These plates fit together like a jigsaw puzzle to form the surface of the earth.

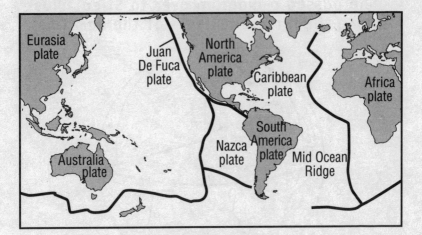

"The plates have been shifting for millions of years. They are, in fact, still shifting. This is what causes earthquakes. The edges of the different plates — called plate margins — are almost always moving, either toward each other, away from each other, or against each other in different directions. They move inches every year — barely noticeable to the human eye.

"As you can imagine, it takes a lot of energy to move a plate a few inches — imagine trying to push a boulder the size of the Pacific Ocean. No one is sure what causes the plates to move. We only know that they *do* move. When plates move apart, a crack opens and molten rock wells up from below, pushing the plates even farther apart. Mostly, this happens on the bottom of oceans. When plates crash together, it is often the case that one plate moves *below* the other. This exerts pressure on the lower lithosphere, causing new rock to rise up — in the form of mountains and volcanoes.

"While earthquakes may happen when plates push apart or crash together, most of them are formed by plates sliding against each other. The rock is under great strain — it is under great pressure to move. Fault lines form at the plate margins. If the plate margins were always perfectly smooth, we wouldn't have any problem — the plates would glide by each other. But plate margins are rarely smooth. Their edges are jagged and interlocking. It is not easy for them to pass one another.

"The plate movement causes stress to build up in the rock. Both plates are pushing against each other. But the energy is not being released. Instead, it builds up. For months, years, even centuries. The rock bends and twists. Then, finally, the energy is too strong. The rock breaks and slips. The energy — all of the energy that has been building up for all this time — is suddenly released in a giant jolt."

"How big of a jolt?" Stieg asked eagerly. Now that we were talking big bangs, he was suddenly interested.

I could tell that Dr. Hoffman noticed this. "The jolt can be stronger than a thousand nuclear bombs," she said. "The moment the energy is released, it breaks free from its core. It travels in shock waves. This is the earthquake.

"The origin of the waves — where the plates have released the energy — is called the focus. The place on the surface of the earth directly above the focus is called the epicenter. The closer the focus is to the epicenter, the smaller the 'felt area' is going to be — this means that the deeper the focus is, the farther the earthquake will spread. Within milliseconds of the quake, the waves travel from the focus. There are three types of waves that are released — primary waves, secondary waves, and surface waves.

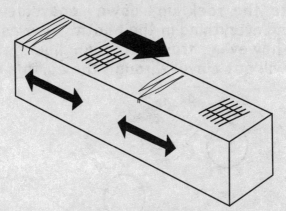

"Primary waves, or P-waves, are the fastest, traveling at five miles a second. They move through the earth the way sound waves travel through air. They emanate from the earthquake's focus, and pressure the parti-

cles in front of them, causing major disturbance and damage.

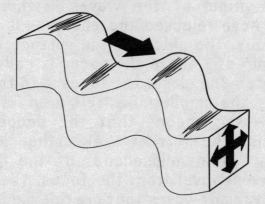

"Secondary waves, also known as S-waves,
travel roughly three miles per second. They
vibrate the rock up, down, and sideways,
shaking everything in their path. S-waves cannot, however, travel through liquid. Thus,
they will not travel through the earth's core.

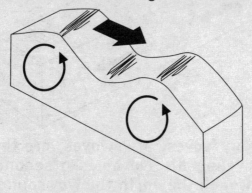

"Surface waves work like waves on the
ocean, causing the ground to rise and fall.

They produce the largest ground motions, even though they only travel on top of the earth, not through it. They travel a little more than two miles per second. They do not occur in all earthquakes. But when they do, the damage can be astonishing.

"Most earthquakes occur in a ring of plate margins around the Pacific Ocean, called the Circumpacific Belt. You are sitting right now atop one of the most active faults in this belt — the San Andreas Fault. San Andreas is the boundary between the Pacific and the North American tectonic plates. Since the Pacific plate is moving northwest and the North American plate is moving south-west, there is a large amount of friction and strain as the two plates move in their opposite directions.

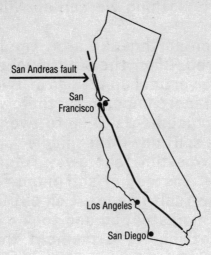

"The San Andreas Fault is millions of years old, and over seven hundred miles long. Some spots are more active than others. For example, in Hollister the fault has been creeping — it moves gradually, sometimes spawning small earthquakes as the plates adjust. This is healthy. The worst thing that can happen along a fault line is nothing. The more time that passes between plate movement, the more energy is being built up for sudden release. It's not a question of whether or not the plates will move — we *know* the plates will move. It's just a matter of when."

"Whoa," Stieg muttered.

"Exactly," Dr. Hoffman said, nodding. "Los Angeles, for example, hasn't had a major earthquake since 1857. But it's sitting on a fault line. The strain is building in the rock beneath it. Nothing we can do will stop the inevitable.

"When an earthquake hits, the land is always altered. After the Great Quake of 1906, there were vertical upheavals of two to three feet. Even more important, there were horizontal displacements of up to twenty feet. A house was split down the middle, and the living room was ten feet away from where it used to be. Instead of shifting a few inches a year, the fault line let it all out at once."

Dr. Hoffman stopped and took a sip of her tea, forgetting for a moment that it had grown cold. I looked at Stieg, who was trans-fixed by her explanations. I wondered if they had an added resonance for him — the un-controllable shifting under the surface, the pressure and the strain leading up to a hor-rific release . . . wasn't this what he was feeling as the Sense pummeled him with warnings? Wasn't this the threat of who he might become?

Dr. Hoffman surprised me with her next words.

"I always told your father not to go near earthquakes," she said calmly, as if she was talking about a diet she'd suggested to him. "They're just too big, too powerful for any of us to fully comprehend. They're the worst of all disasters, in terms of death and destruction. One hundred thousand people killed in Gansu, China, in 1920. Two hundred thousand in Yokohama and Tokyo in 1923. Over fifty-five thousand people in Armenia in 1988. And the Great Quake of 1906 — it doesn't seem as many, only seven hundred. But back then, the population was smaller. Plus, the 1906 quake happened early in the day, when the streets were pretty much empty. Put that quake at rush hour and you get massive carnage."

"So what can be done?" Stieg asked ur-gently.

Dr. Hoffman threw up her hands. "That's

the question, isn't it? We have all sorts of ways to monitor the earth. We have seismograph stations like this one, detecting every little tremor. We track the shape and the level of the ground. We put lasers on fault lines to warn us of even the tiniest of changes. We monitor the water table and sea level changes. We examine the release of radon gas from the earth. We look for changes in gravitational pull and magnetism. We look at historical data.

"Mostly, however, we wait and watch. No one has ever accurately predicted a North American earthquake. Ever."

"Our father did," I said.

"He didn't. The Sense did. Or so everyone says."

"It's going to happen again," Stieg insisted.

Dr. Hoffman smiled. "I know it's going to happen again. We *all* know it's going to happen again. It's just a matter of when. Until you can tell me that, we're still waiting. Ignorantly, desperately waiting."

I wanted to protest. I wanted to yell: *Why aren't you helping us?*

As if she'd read my mind, Dr. Hoffman answered, "There's nothing I can do. Unless Stieg has more to tell us, we'll just have to keep our eye on the fault. And I'll be damn sure to stay away from the carousel."

I looked over to Stieg. I could tell he felt the same way I did.

This wasn't enough.

We had to do more.

Or else.

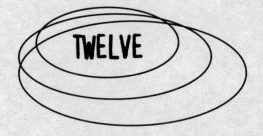

TWELVE

We spent the afternoon walking with Dr. Hoffman, checking out the fault. It could be seen clearly from her kitchen windows — the trees thinned out at the back of the cabin and exposed a rift that ran like a deep scar through the ground.

Dr. Hoffman took us over to see it. Stieg surprised me by bending down and running his hand across the divide. I stared, waiting for a sign of movement in the ground. But it looked as stable as any other part of the landscape.

On our side of the fault sat a laser-ranging electronic distance measurement instrument. Dr. Hoffman explained that it shot a beam to a glass reflector over three thousand feet away. The laser was then reflected back to the instrument, which measured the angle of return. The instrument could detect a shift of as little as .04 inches in the ground level. Any significant shift would be a sign that the plates might be moving — and an earthquake might be near.

That day, however, no shift had been registered.

The same conclusion could be reached by the measure of the water table and gas emissions. Local gravity and magnetism remained constant.

The instruments showed no signs of a quake.

But Stieg knew differently.

Although even he was beginning to doubt it.

"What if I'm wrong?" he asked me when Dr. Hoffman was out of earshot. "What if it's all in my mind?"

"It's not in your mind. It's been in this family for centuries."

"But haven't we ever been wrong? In the Chronicles, aren't there times when the Sense is wrong?"

This was a hard question. Because the answer was yes — sometimes the Sense was wrong. But most of the time it was right. I tried to tell this to Stieg, but he seemed only to hear the first half.

"So it *can* be wrong," he repeated.

"But it isn't. Not this time."

"How can you possibly know that?"

He'd caught me. There was no way for me to know. Like Dr. Hoffman, I was dependent upon science and history for my information. I didn't have the Sense. I didn't have any outside word.

After an hour or two, Dr. Hoffman took us back inside. She showed us her computer room, where she monitored the working seismograph. The seismograph itself was in a concrete-floored vault in a shack beside the cabin. That way it was unlikely to pick up on human disturbances — like Stieg or me walking by. The seismograph registered the vibrations in the earth, and then translated them into a visual record of the waves, called a seismogram. Dr. Hoffman had a simpler seismograph at the edge of her desk — like the ones in her living room, it consisted of a metal arm holding a weighted pen over a rotating scroll of paper. Stieg stared at the fluctuating lines.

"As I told you, the earth is always moving," she said quietly. "The only question is how much. Every year, there are almost a million earthquakes across the planet's surface. A million. Obviously the majority of these aren't major. They are what we call microseisms — little earthquakes. They happen all the time. Then there are man-made disturbances — explosions or drillings — which also shake the earth. They are recorded, too, although they rarely reach a significant magnitude."

Stieg jumped up and down twice; the simple seismograph spiked as he landed. The readout of the computerized seismograph didn't even take notice.

At dinner, Dr. Hoffman tried to get us to talk about ourselves — about our friends, our house, our family. She asked us why we weren't in school, and I told her that the Sense had to come before everything else. She didn't seem to agree with that, but kept her argument to herself.

After dinner, Dr. Hoffman asked me if I wanted to check my E-mail in her office. Stieg went to the guest bedroom to catch up on some reading for school. (He didn't want to do it, but I insisted.) Through intermediaries, I let Grandfather know we were okay. I also looked to see if there were any messages from the Edes. Rachel Ede's disaster sense had been equal to Stieg's when it came to tornadoes. Would the same thing happen with earthquakes? They hadn't E-mailed to let me know of any new developments. Which meant one of two things: They didn't have a clue about the upcoming quake, or they knew and for some reason weren't telling me about it. I wanted to believe the first reason. But the second one gnawed at me more. Whole generations of my family had learned not to trust the Edes. But I'd done exactly the opposite: I'd trusted them. Would I regret it? I wasn't sure.

I sent Rachel and Zach a brief message, telling them where I was and how they could reach me. The best thing would be to force the issue — to ask them point-blank: *Do you know about the earthquake?* But I didn't want to show my hand until I was positive we were still on the same side of the game.

While I was typing, I noticed a red light blinking on Dr. Hoffman's phone. Since Dr. Hoffman was beside me, analzying the day's seismograms, I asked her why the light was lit.

She stared at it curiously and said Stieg must be on the phone.

I was out of my seat in a shot. Who could Stieg be calling?

I ran to the guest bedroom. I didn't bother to knock on the door. Stieg turned to face me, looking guilty. A cordless phone lay belly-up on the bureau next to the bed.

"Who did you call?" I asked, trying — unsuccessfully — to keep the anger out of my voice.

"Just Ben."

Just Ben. From home.

He had called home.

"Why did you call Ben?" I screamed, exasperated.

"Just to get the homework and to say hi."

"And what did you tell him? You're supposed to be home, remember?"

"I know. Don't worry. I told him I was home, sick. I'm sure he believed me."

My head was spinning. Ben was Stieg's best friend. Everybody knew this. It wouldn't be hard for Taggart to learn this. It wouldn't be hard for Taggart to monitor his calls. To track down Stieg's call. To find us here.

"Do you realize what you've done?" I hollered.

"I'm sorry," Stieg said in a small voice. This calmed me down a little. He missed home — I couldn't really blame him for that.

Dr. Hoffman appeared in the doorway behind me.

"I don't think *I* realize what he's done," she said. "If it's about making a long-distance call, that's okay. I can afford a ten-minute call to Connecticut. Just don't call Australia."

"It's not about the phone bill," I said darkly.

Then I had to tell her about Agent Taggart. She didn't seem too worried. I was afraid she thought I was exaggerating the threat.

But I wasn't.

"We have to move," I insisted. Dr. Hoffman disagreed. Stieg didn't say a word.

"There's nowhere to go," Dr. Hoffman argued. "I need to be here with the instruments. But maybe you two should go home. I don't see what good it's doing to have you out here. If there's not going to be an earthquake, you're just wasting time. And if there *is* going to be an earthquake, I don't see what good it does to have you standing in its path. You should go home, where it's safe."

Stieg seemed slightly relieved by her position. But I was petrified. Clearly, the Sense wanted us to stay. We couldn't defy the Sense.

I began to argue, but Dr. Hoffman told me to wait. We would talk about it in the morning. She told me to let Stieg get back to his work. She offered to show me her analysis of the seismograms.

I could tell Stieg wanted me out of the room. So I left — taking the phone with me.

For the next couple of hours, I trawled through a number of quake-related Web sites, trying to see if *anyone* had information about a San Andreas quake. But nobody did. Instead, they made dire predictions about the fate of Los Angeles and Tokyo. The latest buzz was that an earthquake would soon hit Manhattan. It was all very, very scary, even though some of the scientists seemed to be strangely thrilled by the prospect.

Dr. Hoffman read some of the messages over my shoulder. She was not amused.

"Those are the hacks," she said. "Anyone who looks forward to earthquakes couldn't possibly understand them."

I typed away the hours. I lost track of time, but time didn't lose track of me. I was growing tired despite myself. I returned to the guest room to find Stieg sprawled asleep, his fallen books like watchdogs alongside the bed. This meant that I had to sleep on the living room couch. Any other time, I might have woken Stieg up and made him flip a coin for the bed. But I was so happy to see him asleep that I let him lie there undisturbed.

Dr. Hoffman helped me set up the sofa and told me she'd be going to sleep soon, too. Before I could lie down, though, I felt the need to check through the Chronicles one more time.

I returned to the Alaska quake of 1964. Over a million square miles of the earth's surface was affected — the shoreline adjusting by as many as fifteen feet. Three quarters of a billion dollars' worth of property damage was done.

My father and grandfather had been there.

The quake measured 8.4 on the Richter scale, the most devastating American earthquake of the twentieth century. The Richter scale measures the intensity of an earthquake, based on the energy released by the shock. Each number represents ten times more force than the number that precedes it. Thus, the Alaskan quake was ten times more powerful than a 7.5 quake. The San Francisco Quake of 1906 measured 8.3. The other scale by which earthquakes are measured is the Mercalli scale, which gauges actual damage to life and property on a scale of I to XII.

My father couldn't have known the full extent of the damage as he witnessed the quake in Anchorage. He could not have seen firsthand the tidal waves that the earthquake caused, barreling into ports as nearby as Seward (ruining the town and killing thirteen people) and as far away as Japan.

It was Good Friday. 5:36 in the evening. People were getting ready for Easter.

People had no idea what was coming.

Except my father and my grandfather. They knew.

Right after the quake, my father wrote:

It defies belief. Father and I were walking down Fifth Avenue. The trembling began. We fell into the nearest doorway and watched as the streets began to crest and fall. The buildings began to shake apart. All power ceased. There were screams. Glass breaking. In front of my eyes, the cars on the street began to bounce in the air, tires as high as two feet off the ground.

Father began to run. I thought he was crazy. But then I saw where he was running. There was a woman on the sidewalk. A woman with a stroller. A car was headed for her. The driver had lost control. As the woman was knocked to her feet, the stroller began to roll away. Father grabbed it. I rushed out to help him. But the ground wasn't steady. Walls were falling into the street. He pushed the woman out of the way of the car. It bounced past them and crashed into a wall. I ran and pried the driver from his seat. I wasn't *thinking*. I was just *moving*.

I pulled the man from the car. I heard a hideous breaking noise. The wall above the car crashed onto its roof. The earth shook again. I fell over, toppling the man I had saved. Father ran to me, blood on his palms. He asked me if I was okay and when I said I was, he told me to take care of Marta and her baby. I asked him who Marta was. He gestured to the woman and then ran away. He ran twenty feet. I didn't know why. Another wall had fallen. Father was pushing it. He called for me — I could barely hear him, everyone was screaming. I ran. I helped him to push the concrete, but it wouldn't budge. Then I saw the feet in the rubble. We strained. The man from the car joined us. Marta joined us. We pushed aside the wall. But it was too late.

I continued to read — my grandfather's handwriting alongside my father's. The hospital was left without water, heat, or electricity. Doctors and nurses circulated with flashlights, separating the hurt from the dead. More than three quarters of Anchorage was damaged or destroyed. Buildings fell as far as forty feet into the ground. The suburb of Turn-Again-by-the-Sea literally fell *into* the sea. Elsewhere, hills were cleaved by avalanches. Mud erupted from holes in the earth.

I pored through the Chronicle entries. They fascinated me. They enthralled me. But I had to wonder — would they really help? When the earth began to tear itself apart — when the walls began to tumble and the cars skidded out of control — what could the Chronicles say that would help me? If anything, they made it painstakingly clear: The Atwood "gift" was for predicting disasters, not necessarily for battling them. At most, the Sense told us the time and place. But once we got there, we were merely human.

I read the Chronicles well past midnight. I was still searching — for the secret spell that could make things go away. For the key to courage. For the hope that no one would die.

But I couldn't find any of these things. I couldn't find any guarantees. For every few lives that were saved, there always seemed to be a person in the rubble. For every few moments of *right on time*, there was at least one moment of *too late*.

I put the Chronicles away for the night, hoping the stories would not turn my sleep to nightmares. Stieg's nightmares.

On my way to the bathroom, I passed Stieg's door. I half-expected to hear him rustling and restless, but the quality of the silence led me to believe he was asleep.

The light was still on in Dr. Hoffman's office. I poked my head in and saw her sitting in a nightgown at her desk. "Come in," she said, motioning me through the doorway. "I always say I'm going to sleep, but there's always too much to do."

I walked in. Above the desk were two telltale lines I'd noticed earlier:

Oh, these little earthquakes.
Doesn't take much to rip us into pieces.

"It's from a Tori Amos song," Dr. Hoffman explained.

"It fits," I said, thinking of Stieg.

Dr. Hoffman nodded. "I remember when your mother first realized that Stieg had the Sense. When he was — what? — eighteen months old? She had thought it would be you. But then it became clear that Stieg was the one. She wasn't too thrilled about it. It was hard enough having a husband with the Sense. But a son — with all of the risks involved — that was worse. The saving grace was that she felt she would be here when the time came for Stieg to deal with the Sense, that he would be with his father, as his father had been with your grandfather at first. And of course . . . well, that hasn't happened."

We sat in silence for a moment, both of us

thinking of my parents, no doubt in different ways.

One of the cats came creeping into the room, jumping right onto Dr. Hoffman's lap. Dr. Hoffman stroked her gently and asked her quietly about earthquakes.

"The animals are our best indicator," Dr. Hoffman explained to me. "Simone here is a better predictor of earthquakes than any other instrument in this room. Animal behavior has been known to alter considerably before quakes. Cows refuse to go into barns. Rats stagger drunkenly. Reptiles emerge from hibernation months before they are supposed to."

"Is that why you have cats?" I asked.

Dr. Hoffman smiled. "No. I have cats because I love them. Sometimes I fear they are much better companions than people. Present company excluded, of course. My love for cats put a great strain between me and your mother, since she was so allergic. But, as with most things, we found a way to compromise."

Dr. Hoffman was about to continue, but she was stopped by a sudden crash. I jumped out of my seat, expecting the earth to tremble and the walls to cave in. There was another crash — this time more of a thud.

"What is that?" I asked.
It wasn't coming from the ground.
It was coming from another room.
Another crash. Pictures falling from a wall.
Stieg's room.

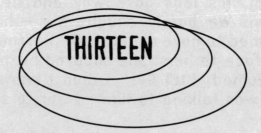

THIRTEEN

The first thing I saw was the blood. Then I saw my brother's body hit the wall. As if it had been thrown. His eyes were closed. His nose was bleeding and his lip was cut. His hand hit the wall first. Then the rest of his body followed, with a sickening thud.

He didn't fall. He clung to the wall for a second. Then he fell backward, crashing into a chest of drawers. Dr. Hoffman and I ran over to him. He was trying to stand up. I tried to encircle him in my arms, but he pulled away. He was pulled away. As if gravity had shifted. He stumbled back into the wall. His body was pressed against the wood. He began to walk. Still pressed against the wall, he sleepily dragged his face across the grain, leaving an eerie, bloody trail.

We stopped him. Dr. Hoffman and I both

grabbed him. Together, we wrenched him from the wall. He was moving in many directions at once. His arms didn't seem connected. One reached up, the other one down. His legs gave way and he tumbled down. We barely caught him — his weight seemed to have doubled. Dr. Hoffman turned his face to hers. She shouted his name. She screamed, "LET GO!" I didn't know whether she was talking to him . . . or to something else.

When his convulsions had stopped, I ran to the bathroom in search of a first-aid kit. From the hallway, I heard Stieg begin to whimper. The sound chilled me to the bone.

Armed with supplies, I returned to the room. Stieg's crying had stopped almost as soon as it had started. Now he looked angry and bewildered.

"You're lucky you didn't break your wrist," Dr. Hoffman said, examining Stieg's cuts and bruises.

"What happened?" I asked.

"You tell me," he replied.

"The Sense?"

"You get an A-plus on this exam."

"What did you see?"

He winced as Dr. Hoffman put ointment on his forehead, where he'd opened a cut a few millimeters above his eye. "I saw the amusement park," he said. "I was on a roller coaster and my seat belt broke. I was hurtling through the sky and suddenly everyone else had fallen off. You were there. We were all falling. Then we hit. The ground was shaking. People were jumping from the top of the Ferris wheel. I was running to catch them. But the ground was moving too fast. I kept falling. I kept hitting walls."

"When was it?" I asked.

"What do you mean?"

"What time of the day was it? Was it day? Night?"

"It was day."

"Morning or afternoon?"

"I don't know. Late morning, I think. Why would anyone be at an amusement park early in the morning?"

I thought about this for a second. It gave me another idea.

"Were there kids there?" I inquired. "Besides you and me."

"Sure," Stieg answered. I could tell he thought it was a strange question.

"Are you positive?"

"Yeah. There were lots of them."

Dr. Hoffman had stopped tending to Stieg's wounds. Now she looked at me.

"Are you saying what I think you're saying?" she asked.

"Will somebody please tell me what you're talking about?" Stieg insisted.

"Your nightmares are giving us clues, in the details," I explained. "If the things you saw happened during the day, that means the earthquake will probably hit during the day. And if you saw plenty of kids at the amusement park, that means it will probably hit over the weekend. If it were during the week, kids would be in school."

"So we have another day," Stieg said. We had already passed midnight and entered into Friday.

"We don't know that it's going to happen *this* weekend," Dr. Hoffman cautioned. "Or *any* weekend. We can't shut down the state of California because Stieg's had a nightmare, no matter how horrible it was."

Stieg's nose had begun to bleed again. I handed him a tissue. He paused for a moment, letting the blood trickle to his broken lip.

"Stieg?" I asked.

His look was far away.

He blinked and held the tissue to his nose.

"What?" he asked. Wherever he'd gone, he wasn't going to tell me about it. Or maybe he couldn't.

As Stieg sat on the floor, Dr. Hoffman and I straightened up the room. Some of the picture frames had been smashed. Slivers of glass were sprinkled across the hardwood floor. I quickly inspected Stieg's socks; luckily, none of the glass had broken through. I tried to remember if the Sense had ever treated its host so roughly. But I couldn't remember a single instance from the Chronicles involving anything like this. Maybe it wasn't the Sense that had caused it. Maybe it was the dangerous intersection of the Sense and this particular Atwood.

Clearly, the Sense would not be ignored. It would make itself heard . . . no matter what.

But what was it saying?

I wasn't sure that Stieg knew.

We finished cleaning the room. After we'd gotten Stieg back to bed and we'd said our cautious good nights, Stieg spoke his final words of the night:

"We'll have to be in the amusement park when the quake hits," he whispered as I left the room.

I didn't know whether I was supposed to have heard him.

But I did.

FOURTEEN

Stieg came to breakfast the next morning looking like he'd gotten into a fight with a wall — and lost. Which wasn't too far from the truth.

"One more day until the weekend," he said. We all knew what he meant.

I stood up to get him some orange juice. At the refrigerator, I paused. Dr. Hoffman had hung a bizarre drawing on its front, with various animals balanced in strange positions. I asked her what it meant.

Dr. Hoffman smiled at my question.

"Before plate tectonics were understood," she explained, "there were a variety of theories about the origins of earthquakes. Some of them date as far back as history has been recorded. The most consistent belief was that the earth was held on the back of a giant animal; when the animal moved, an earthquake occurred. Some Hindus believed an elephant supported the earth; others argued that it was a mole. Algonquins placed the planet on the back of a huge tortoise — earthquakes occurred when the tortoise shifted its weight around.

"The drawing on the refrigerator is based on the beliefs of one early East African tribe. They believed the earth was balanced on the horn of a huge cow, which was itself perched on a rock that lay on the back of a fish swimming in an ocean. Earthquakes occurred when the cow grew tired, and shifted the weight of the world from one horn to another.

"Another group — this time in India — believed that the earth was supported by seven snakes, which held the planet in shifts. When the world was passed from one snake to another, an earthquake occurred."

"Why are there seven snakes?" Stieg asked. "Why not eight, or eleven?"

Dr. Hoffman shook her head. "Nobody knows."

"But everyone thought that the earth was balanced by an animal?"

"Not everyone," Dr. Hoffman corrected. "Some cultures believed that earthquakes were caused by creatures *on* the earth. On the Indonesian island of Sulawesi, it was said

113

that earthquakes were caused by a giant hog that occasionally stopped to rub its back against an even larger tree. Various factions in Japan argued that earthquakes were caused by either a twitching whale, a walking spider, or a prankster catfish. The giant catfish — called the *namazu* — was said to live in the mud beneath the earth. Only the god Kashima, who protected Japan from earthquakes, could stop it from shaking the world apart.

"The Greek philosopher Aristotle wrote that quakes happened when all of the water and air that were daily absorbed by the earth decided that it wanted to come back out again. More recently, people have believed that earthquakes are punishments for evil deeds. But I don't believe that. Not one bit. I'm more inclined to believe that we are, in fact, being balanced on the horn of a cow."

I brought the orange juice to the table.

"So what's next?" Stieg asked.

Dr. Hoffman sighed. "I know you're not going to like this, but I think it's necessary. As I said last night, I think the two of you should go home. There's nothing for you to do here. You're both very smart and brave. But the bottom line is that you are both children. If an earthquake is going to occur, there is no need for you to be caught in the middle of it. So I'm going to take you to the airport and send you back to your grandfather. I called him this morning and he agreed."

"You called him? From *here*?" I asked, not believing it.

Dr. Hoffman shook her head. "You've managed to make me more than a little paranoid. So I went into town while you were still sleeping. As I said, your grandfather agreed with me. It's becoming too much. You should go home."

Stieg surprised me with the vehemence of his next words. "That's not an option," he stated firmly. "We can't leave. It won't let me leave."

"What do you mean?" Dr. Hoffman asked, looking deeply into Stieg's eyes. I looked, too. Stieg's gaze was made of steel. Unbendable. Unfeeling.

"We have to be here," he replied. "I can't explain how I know this. I just do. We can't leave. Or, at least, *I* can't leave."

He didn't turn to look at me. He didn't even acknowledge that I was in the room. But there it was: He was saying I wasn't necessary. I could leave. He was the essential one. He would have to stay.

"No way," I exclaimed. "We're in this together."

Stieg didn't put up an argument. He remained silent.

"Why are you saying this?" Dr. Hoffman asked Stieg seriously. "Are you speaking for yourself, or for the Sense? Don't you want to go home? Don't you want to be back with your friends?"

"I want to," Stieg said quietly. "But I can't. I have to stay."

Dr. Hoffman slammed her hand on the counter. The glasses jumped. I was startled. Stieg seemed to understand.

"I don't know what to do," Dr. Hoffman said, mostly to herself.

"We're staying," Stieg answered gently. "We'll stay until it's over."

And that was it. We were staying.

Until it was over.

We spent the day checking the instruments, looking for a sign — *any* sign — of seismological activity. But the ground moved to its usual rhythms. Gas emissions, water tables, and magnetism remained normal. The fault showed no sign of disruption. The seismographs monitored impassively. There was no cause for alarm. Except for what the Sense was saying.

I read the Chronicles until I was tired of reading. Exasperated, I shoved them out of sight, beneath the couch. They weren't helping. They were answering the *what* instead of the *when*. We were all tiptoeing around the *when*, afraid of waking it up and turning it into a *now*. And at the same time we secretly wanted *now* to arrive, just so we could act, instead of waiting.

Stieg insisted that we had to go to the amusement park early the next morning — to warn people away — to be there when it happened. Dr. Hoffman joined me in shooting down this idea. If we tried to warn people, we'd probably be arrested. And if we were there during the quake, we might be killed.

Our periodic arguments punctuated the unbearable length of the day. Stieg threatened to run off to the amusement park. Dr. Hoffman threatened to send us home. I threatened to lock Stieg in his room. We were getting on each other's nerves.

And still the instruments showed no sign of disturbance.

Stieg remained unsteady. His bruised condition made matters worse. He tried to take a nap, but couldn't — he felt the bed was on top of him, instead of vice versa.

At dinner, one of the cats sprang onto the table. All three of us jumped, thinking the quake had arrived.

Things were not good.

I caught Stieg staring in the bathroom

mirror. He was giving himself a look of pure hatred. As if he could be blamed for having the Sense. As if he could blame himself.

I told him to stop being angry.

He walked right past me. He closed the door to the guest room as I approached.

The day was long. But eventually it ended.

At night, the three of us watched TV without saying a word. Dr. Hoffman left every few minutes to check the seismograph. She told us she had called the manager of Wonder World, an old acquaintance of hers. While she didn't actually tell the manager that there was going to be a quake, she lied and said she'd seen small signs of a possible quake, and that the amusement park should be prepared for such a disaster. The manager assured her the employees were well trained for a "quake scenario." This made Dr. Hoffman feel a little better — but not much. I said it was a start. Stieg didn't seem to be playing attention.

The cats began to meow. All at once. I checked the window to see if anyone was coming. I made sure their bowls were filled. When Dr. Hoffman returned to the room, I asked her what was going on.

"I don't know," she said, bone-tired. "It could be tomorrow. Or it could be the tension in this house. Cats pick up on that."

She turned off the TV. Very solemnly, she told us that our situation had to change. We couldn't work this way. If there *was* an earthquake coming tomorrow, or the day after, the three of us would have to work as a team.

"I have to hope," she concluded, "we've gotten all of this bickering out of our system. Tomorrow we'll have to work together."

"Then we'll go to the amusement park?" Stieg asked.

Dr. Hoffman shook her head. Stieg looked away.

The TV was turned back on. But it didn't really matter. Our minds were elsewhere. We were buried under thoughts of tomorrow. We could have shared them with each other. But we didn't.

Stieg said he was tired and that he was going to try to go to bed. We asked him to keep the door open, so we could hear if anything happened. He agreed.

Dr. Hoffman went again to check the instruments. I sat back on the couch. I didn't mean to go to sleep, but I guess I did. Because the next thing I remember is being awakened by a sharp knock on the door.

Once. Twice. It sounded as if someone was trying to kick the door in.

I was jolted upright. Dr. Hoffman came into the room from the other direction, turning on the lights.

"Who is it?" she asked. I looked at the clock. It was six in the morning.

The door burst open. Dr. Hoffman fell back.

I stood up . . . and came face to face with Agent Taggart.

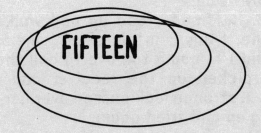

FIFTEEN

I expected more agents to come pouring in. I expected a full SWAT team to burst through the door.

But no.

Agent Taggart was alone.

And he wasn't very happy.

It took a moment for Dr. Hoffman to regain her voice. When she did, it was clear that *she* wasn't very happy, either.

"What do you think you're doing?" she yelled.

Taggart flashed his badge and introduced himself. He apologized for kicking in the door.

"I was afraid you wouldn't let me in," he said, looking around.

Looking for Stieg.

"Where's the other kid?" he asked.

Dr. Hoffman and I turned to each other. We didn't say a word.

"Very funny," Taggart barked, in a way that made it clear he didn't think it was funny at all.

Dr. Hoffman stood up and walked to the phone. "This is intolerable," she said. "I'm afraid I'm going to have to call the police." She picked up the receiver and began to dial. A strange look passed over her face. She hung up and tried again.

"I'm afraid you won't be calling anyone right now," Taggart spoke, sounding genuinely apologetic.

"The phones are dead," Dr. Hoffman said softly.

"I know that, ma'am."

I stared at Taggart. This was beginning to seem insane. Even *I* knew that agents from the U.S. Weather Service — or wherever it was that he came from — didn't go barging into homes, cutting the phone lines, and barking commands.

Dr. Hoffman knew this, too. It was clear she wasn't going to give up without a fight. But at the same time, she knew she wouldn't necessarily win.

We *both* knew we wouldn't necessarily win.

"Get Stieg," Taggart ordered. *"Now."*

He pulled a gun from his holster, to emphasize his point.

This is not happening, I thought to myself. *This is just a nightmare. I haven't really woken up yet.*

I walked through the dark hallway to get Stieg. I hit my knee on a chair.

It hurt.

I was awake.

This was really happening.

I could hear Dr. Hoffman begin to argue with Agent Taggart. I could hear him assure her that nothing harmful was going to happen. He just needed to know why we were here, and what we were up to. Stieg's door was open, as we had arranged. I looked into the darkness. It was so quiet — it seemed a shame to wake him. I whispered his name, trying to be gentle. No response. I reached for the light switch and tried to find his body in the bed. But I couldn't see a thing. I turned on the light.

Stieg wasn't there.

I called out his name, louder now. Still no response. I ran to the bed. The sheets were rumpled. The blanket had fallen to the floor.

Stieg was nowhere to be found.

I looked under the bed, perversely thinking that maybe he had fallen there in his sleep. I looked in the closet. I looked under the desk.

Nothing.

I ran to the bathroom, thinking he had

woken up and gone there. But the light was off and the room was empty.

"What's going on?!?" Taggart yelled from the den.

I had no idea what my answer would be.

I checked Dr. Hoffman's study. I checked her bedroom. I looked out the window.

Nothing.

I checked the kitchen. Agent Taggart was calling for me again. I yelled that I would be there in a moment. But he beat me to it. He burst into the room, pulling Dr. Hoffman in behind him.

"Why are you in here?" he yelled.

"I can't find him," I confessed.

"*What?*"

"I can't find him. He's supposed to be sleeping in his room. But he's not."

"Show me."

I led the way. But really, it was Taggart who led the way, with his gun. He was the one causing the movement. I was just pointing out the direction.

Stieg still wasn't there. I was distressed, because I knew Taggart wouldn't take the news lightly.

I was also glad. Because maybe, just maybe, Stieg had gotten away.

"I can't believe this!" Taggart hollered. "He's the one I need, right? He's the one who knows."

I didn't have anything to say to that.

"Stieg!" Taggart yelled. "I'm only here to help. I have your brother and your friend here. It would be best if you would come here and talk with us. I only want to talk. We're on the same side, you know. We both want to prevent the disaster that's about to hit. That's what you want, right? That's what I want, too."

No answer.

"This doesn't have to be hard," Taggart continued. His voice lost a little of its confidence with each sentence; he knew it wasn't working. "Your parents were very cooperative. I helped them to save many lives. Now it's your turn to work with me. I don't know what you and your grandfather are so afraid of. You didn't need to have those people come down on me. I was only doing my job. I'm still doing my job. So please, just come here."

Taggart was turning his body as he spoke, shouting to every corner of the house. I wanted to tell him it was too late. I wanted to tell him to give up. Stieg was more stubborn than the rest of us combined.

Taggart raised his gun and fired a shot into the ceiling. Dr. Hoffman and I jumped. Taggart put out his hand, to calm us down.

"Don't worry," he said. "That was just for show."

"How dare you!" Dr. Hoffman yelled. "This is *crazy*. I demand that you put that gun down this instant. I would like to see your authorization. I would like to talk to your superior. And, most of all, I would like you to leave my house *right now*."

"You think this is crazy?" Taggart asked, giving Dr. Hoffman an incredulous look. "This isn't crazy. Crazy is when an eleven-year-old boy can predict the weather. Crazy is when a little brat has a power that governments and kingdoms have been trying to harness since the beginning of time. And he won't even co-operate!"

Agent Taggart raised his gun. Although it wasn't pointed at me or Dr. Hoffman, the threat was there.

"Call your brother," he ordered. "And make it good."

I gave it my full-force, Oscar-performance best, shouting Stieg's name at the top of my lungs. Taggart seemed satisfied. He didn't realize that Stieg rarely came when I called. I doubted he would start listening now.

Taggart put the gun back down and told Dr. Hoffman and me to return to the den. I could see Dr. Hoffman looking around. I guessed she was trying to come up with an escape plan. She was too cautious to make a half-hearted attempt.

In truth, Taggart didn't seem very interested in the two of us. It was clear that Stieg was his great reward.

I remembered some of the things my parents had written in the Chronicles about Taggart. They had never told him about the Sense. In the beginning, he hadn't even suspected it — he simply thought that my parents had a natural ability to predict the weather. Then after a while, he became suspicious. He hounded them and had them watched. He pressured them into more and more dangerous situations. My parents felt trapped. Even though Taggart didn't know everything, he knew too much. He threatened to make it public. He threatened to ruin their lives, just as he was threatening to ruin ours.

"Just keep calm," Dr. Hoffman whispered to me. "He's not going to hurt us. There's no reason for him to hurt us. We just have to play along."

While Taggart searched Stieg's room one more time, Dr. Hoffman asked me if I knew where Stieg really was.

I had to answer no.

"Are you sure?" Taggart asked. I was startled — I hadn't realized he was listening.

"I'm sure," I replied. It helped that it was the truth.

Dr. Hoffman and I were seated on the couch. Taggart pulled up a chair and sat facing us.

"So when's it going to happen?" he asked.

"Today," I answered with more authority than I felt.

"An earthquake?"

I nodded.

"Here?"

I nodded again.

"How do you know?"

"We just know." I sighed.

"What time?"

"During the day."

"More specific?"

I shook my head.

"Good enough." Taggart slapped his leg and pulled out a cellular phone. Within moments, he had speed-dialed someone, I assumed in Washington, D.C.

"Taggart here," he began. "Yes . . . no . . . look, listen to me — I have news. . . . An earthquake, near San Francisco. . . . No, I'm not crazy. . . . No, this is for real. . . . What do you mean, you can't do anything? . . . I have reliable sources. . . . No, they're not scientific. . . . No, I haven't bothered the kid. . . . What do you mean? . . . *Take it under advisement?* Do you understand what I'm saying? Do you have the faintest clue as to what I'm saying? You have to evacuate. You have to begin the warnings. *Now.* What? What? *NO I WON'T HOLD!"*

Taggart threw the phone across the room. It crashed against the wall.

Dr. Hoffman and I sat in a shocked silence. Taggart paced the room maniacally.

Taggart's superiors obviously didn't believe in him as much as he believed in the Sense.

We passed a few minutes in silence. I listened to the other rooms of the house, for any small movement that might point to Stieg. But everything was quiet, except for the cats. Outside the windows, the sun began to rise.

I kept wondering where Stieg had gone.

I kept thinking: *the amusement park.*

Taggart sat down again. He had returned his gun to its holster. This made me feel a little better.

Dr. Hoffman shifted on the sofa. I could tell she was preparing to speak.

"You've gotten what you came for," she said, very calmly, to Taggart. "As you said, we can all work together. I have many important seismographic instruments that I am supposed to monitor. I would like to check them. I would also like for you to let us go. Clearly, we want the same thing — to minimize the damage from the earthquake that may or may not happen today. Let us do that."

"You're right," Taggart replied, "and you're wrong. I thank you for your information and, yes, I want to save lives. But I also want something more. Can't you understand that, Dr. Seismologist? I want the kid. I want to see what makes the whole thing work. I want to have his power under my command — under the *government's* command."

I didn't say a word. I felt ashamed of my silence — if Stieg had been there, he would have been yelling at Taggart, telling him to take a long leap off a high bridge. But the only way I could think to refuse him was to keep my mouth shut.

"I've seen your file, Dr. Hoffman," Taggart continued. "I don't know if you're fully aware of the power these kids have. Imagine a seismograph that could predict the future. Imagine a weather radar that was set an hour ahead of schedule. It would change the world. That is the power that these kids have. And their parents had. And many of their ancestors had. I don't know the full scope of it. But I'm sure it's awesome." Taggart turned to me. "Isn't that right, Adam?"

I didn't say a word.

Taggart was amused by this. "Not talking, are we? Well, tell me this: Are there any written records of the Atwood family heroics? I asked your grandfather, but he wasn't very helpful. So now I'm asking you."

The fact that Taggart had to ask the question meant that he probably didn't know the answer. He didn't know about the Chronicles. I thought about the volumes I had pushed under the sofa — could he really not see them? They were inches away from my feet. They were inches away from his sight line.

And still, I lied.

"No," I answered. "We don't write anything down. That way we can't be caught."

"Ah, but you *can* be caught," Taggart observed smugly. Then he stood up. "I guess we should check the instruments."

We did a full tour of the seismographs, lasers, and sensors. As before, there was no sign of suspicious activity — only the cats' strange behavior, which was growing in intensity as our situation worsened.

It took hours for Dr. Hoffman to make all of her measurements. She was extra attentive — she was looking for some sign, *any* sign, that Stieg was right. Taggart seemed lulled into complacence by Dr. Hoffman's calculations. Still, he wouldn't let either of us out of his sight.

I kept listening for Stieg. The longer he was gone, the surer I was that he had gotten far away. Because I felt that if Stieg was around, I would know it. If he was around, the same brotherly intuition that had allowed me to find him when we played hide-and-seek would give away his present location. Now I felt he was out of range. On the road. On his way to the one place he wanted to be: Wonder World.

Taggart asked me more questions about the Sense. I answered him vaguely. I told him I didn't know that much about it. I pointed out that I was only fourteen. He liked to see us as kids, so I let him think we were as mindless as that label allowed.

I wondered how Taggart had found us. Was it Stieg's phone call to Ben? Dr. Hoffman's phone call to Grandfather? No one knew our whereabouts. No one except Tinka, Mrs. Amata . . . and the Edes. In my E-mail, I had told the Edes where we were. Had they somehow turned us in? I found this hard to believe. I had decided to trust Rachel and Zach. I thought I'd had good reason to trust them. But maybe they had only been nice to us when it was their own house that was at risk. Or maybe their parents had somehow intercepted my message. . . .

"What is it? Are you getting premonitions?" Agent Taggart interrupted, successfully derailing my train of thought.

"How did you find us?" I asked.

Taggart grinned.

"I have my ways," he replied, self-satisfied. That was all he'd tell me. I guess he wanted my suspicions to go wild.

I couldn't get the questions out of my mind:

How had he known?

Who had told?

As I sank further into my chair, Dr. Hoffman checked the seismograph on her computer. She was unable to use her modem, since Taggart had cut the phone lines.

"It would really help to communicate with other observatories," she insisted.

Taggart, staring over her shoulder, wouldn't budge.

"You'll have to make do with what you have."

This clearly got under Dr. Hoffman's skin. She pushed the keyboard away and stood up, locking eyes with a fairly surprised Taggart.

"Look," she spat, "this is ridiculous. You are interfering with my work. I cannot stand for that. If you are truly concerned about the well-being of others, you will let me use all available resources. Right now, you are little more than a bully and a nuisance."

Taggart pushed her back into her seat. Hard. Dr. Hoffman landed with a thud. Taggart raised his hand. I jumped up. For a moment, I thought he was going to hit her. She thought so, too, moving to shield herself. But instead of striking her, Taggart stepped back.

"Sit down!" he barked at me.

I sat down.

"Why are you doing this?" Dr. Hoffman asked.

This request for an explanation seemed to calm Taggart down a little bit. He seemed to forget that he had just pushed Dr. Hoffman. She, however, didn't.

"Why am I doing this?" Taggart echoed. "Well, let me tell you a story. It's not a story you're likely to have heard before. I grew up on a farm in Nebraska. I worked hard, I behaved well, and I expected life would be kind to me. Then, one April, the sky turned gray. I was alone in the house — my parents had gone to town for supplies. The tornado hit before I could realize what was happening. I was thrown to the ground. I watched as our barn was torn apart. It was over in a matter of seconds. Suddenly, the wind was gone. I pulled myself up and went running down the road. I was running to the neighbors, to see if they were okay. But something stopped me. I saw my parents' car, lying on the side of the road, upside down. It had been thrown into a pair of trees. I screamed so loudly that people heard me a mile away. I ran to the car. But it was too late."

"I'm sorry," Dr. Hoffman whispered.

"Don't be. It's not *your* fault."

Taggart paused and turned to me. "So you see, you and I aren't so different after all. But my story isn't over yet. Three towns over, my second cousins were sitting down to lunch. A stranger came up to their door and told them to run to the cellar. He said his name was Edward, and that a twister was coming. Something in his voice made them listen. They ran to the cellar and bolted the door. The stranger wouldn't come with them; he had other people to warn. Sure enough, within minutes, my second cousins heard the violent howl of the tornado, right over their heads. When they finally left the cellar, they found that most of their house had been destroyed. The stranger had saved their lives.

"Now, if I'm not mistaken, your grandfather's name was Edward. And, I believe, he was in Nebraska at the time of the tornado. There's no proof of this; I just happen to think it was so. And I still wonder why a man who knew a tornado was coming wouldn't have broadcast it to all the counties. Why didn't he work with the government and warn everyone? What right did he have to warn my second cousins and not my parents? Who gave him the power to play God?"

Taggart glared at me, as if I had the answers. But I didn't. I only knew this: Taggart had driven my parents to their graves. And that was before he knew the full scope of the Sense. He was sure to strain Stieg even harder. Stieg would become a lab rat. He would lose all his freedom. And maybe even his life. Taggart would push the Sense too far — it would cross the breaking point and disappear.

There was no way to tell any of this to Taggart. That would be admitting too much. Because even if I told him the Sense would go away, he would want to try. Stieg's freedom wasn't worth anything to him. My parents' freedom hadn't mattered to him. Neither had their lives.

Taggart sighed. "Eventually your brother will come back," he stated. "Then we will return to D.C. and this whole affair will be over. My superiors will have the *evidence* they have been hounding me for. When this earthquake hits, they will know that I had predicted it. They will regret that they ever hung up on me."

"What if it doesn't hit?" I asked.

"We both know that it's going to hit," Taggart replied. Then his smile froze on his face. "If you're lying," he growled, "your punishment will be extreme."

"I'm not lying," I assured him. But my

voice sounded weak. I was afraid he didn't believe me.

"Leave him alone," Dr. Hoffman demanded.

"Shut up and focus on your computer," Taggart yelled.

"How long are we going to be held like this?" she asked.

"As long as it takes, sweetheart."

I think it was this last *sweetheart* that set her off. I could tell from the look in her eyes. She wasn't going to take this much longer. She was just looking for her moment.

Three of the cats ran into the room. They were as restless as ever.

Dr. Hoffman bent down to pet them. They continued to screech and wrestle.

"They're hungry," Dr. Hoffman told Taggart. "I have to feed them."

"Will they be quiet, then?"

Dr. Hoffman nodded.

"Okay," Taggart decided. "Let's go."

We walked to the kitchen together, Taggart's gun still within his reach. Dr. Hoffman was way deeper in thought than a trip to feed the cats deserved. Taggart didn't seem to notice.

I looked for a sign — a gesture or a word from her, telling me what to do. Taggart and I watched as she bent down to get the bag of cat food. Ten bowls — five for water, five for food — sat at her feet. It all seemed so normal. Then Dr. Hoffman did something strange: Instead of reaching for the opened bag of cat food, she pulled a new one out of the cupboard. It was one of those bulk bags of pet food, roughly the size of a sandbag.

Dr. Hoffman lifted the bag and shot me a look. At once, I knew what to do. I fell to my knees, crashing loudly to the floor. Startled, Taggart turned to me. "What the —" he began, reaching for his holster with one hand and holding out the other to me. Dr. Hoffman raised the bag of cat food and swung it squarely against the side of Taggart's head. He buckled forward, crying out in pain. I lunged for his legs, bringing him down. Dr. Hoffman swung again and Taggart hit the counter. Hard.

"LET'S GO!" Dr. Hoffman yelled. I lifted myself past Taggart and ran for the door. Dr. Hoffman bent over to pick something up — Taggart's phone. In the kitchen, he groaned. Dr. Hoffman and I bolted out of the house, tore through the clearing and onto the path. I could hear Taggart yelling behind us. I turned back — he was stumbling out of the doorway, gun raised.

A shot. Nowhere near us. But still — a shot.

I followed Dr. Hoffman through the trees. She pushed aside branches — they sprang back into my face. I didn't care. I just ran. I could hear Taggart shouting. He was behind us. He was following the path. More branches. The sound of Dr. Hoffman panting — I was losing breath — we were too loud. We pushed forward. I don't know what gave me such strength. I'd never run faster in my life.

We reached the road.

Left, right, or forward? Dr. Hoffman stopped for moment, then pulled me to the left. Taggart's car was in front of us. A rental — it had to be his. We ran to the yard on the other side of the road. We were visible. I didn't look back. We ran through the yard into another set of woods. We were under cover again. Dr. Hoffman slowed her pace. I gasped for breath. We looked back. Taggart was coming down the path. Taggart had reached his car. He seemed as exhausted as we were. He looked around. He held his hand to his brow, blocking out the sun. He looked for us. We were quiet — so quiet. He looked in our direction, but only for a moment. His gaze moved right on past.

He didn't see us.

After a minute or two, he slammed his fist onto the hood of his car. He shouted curses. He pointed his gun. He looked again.

He still didn't see us.

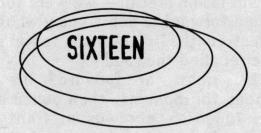

SIXTEEN

We pulled back deeper into the woods, careful of our every step.

Soon, Taggart disappeared from view. The trees were a solid wall between us. Dr. Hoffman began to walk faster. I followed.

"Where are we going?" I asked.

"Where do you think your brother is?"

"The amusement park."

"Exactly."

I gestured back in Taggart's direction. "Do you think he'll follow us?"

"Absolutely."

Dr. Hoffman opened up Taggart's cellular phone and punched in a few numbers.

"What are you doing?" I asked, still catching my breath. "They could trace your call."

Dr. Hoffman shook her head. "Do you see any other phone available?"

The answer was clearly no. We were in the heart of Randall's Peak, far away from all the other houses. The land was starting to slant — we were walking down the mountain, straight for Wonder World.

"Hello?" Dr. Hoffman said into the receiver. "Yes — I need to talk to Shelly Eberhard. . . . No, I can't hold. . . . *Yes*, it's an emergency. This is Dr. Hoffman, from the Peak. . . . Hello? Shelly — yes, I'm afraid something's happened. Nothing definite, but some signs . . . yes. Look — I need you to do something. . . . No — I know you can't shut down the park. But maybe the most dangerous rides . . . Yes, I understand. But that's not what I need you to do. I need you to find someone for me. His name is Stieg Atwood. . . . Stieg — it rhymes with league. . . . Yes, page him and have him meet us at the gate. . . . No, I'm not home. I'm on a cell phone. I'm coming down — I should be there in a few minutes. . . . Okay. 'Bye."

She put the phone back in her pocket.

"Can you run again?" she asked.

"I can try," I replied.

She picked up the pace. We ran. Which would have been hard enough for me on an even surface. Going downhill in a steep forest was even worse. I kept tripping on stones. I kept falling into branches. But the faster I moved, the more I knew that I had to move even faster. I didn't have to look at my watch to know that time was running out.

We stumbled down the way. Finally, we hit a winding road. We peered cautiously from between the trees. There were no cars in sight.

"Almost there," Dr. Hoffman assured me. "You're doing great."

I didn't feel great.

I felt as if all of the air were bleeding out of my body.

We continued to run.

Houses appeared more frequently. We ran through their backyards. A few people yelled at us. We ignored them. The background sounds changed. The cool quiet of the trees gave way to the cotton-candy sounds of the amusement park. The mass of screams and laughter. The PA system Muzak. The steamroller glide of the roller coaster.

The fence was within view.

"What are we going to do?" I rasped between breaths.

"First, we find Stieg," Dr. Hoffman answered. "The rest . . . we'll have to see."

We were in the parking lot. We had to stop running — we were too exhausted. Dr. Hoffman called the amusement park manager again and asked her if Stieg had been found.

There had been no sign of him. Not yet.

Shelly Eberhard met us at the gate. We were waved in ahead of the line. I wanted to tell everyone to go away. I wanted to warn them away from the earthquake. But I kept quiet. I still wasn't sure.

Ms. Eberhard took us to her office. She said she had paged Stieg numerous times; he hadn't responded.

There were only two explanations, in my mind: Either Stieg thought it was Agent Taggart paging him, or he wasn't in the amusement park at all.

Either way, we were stuck.

"Now what's this all about, Piper?" Ms. Eberhard demanded.

"I told you — I have reason to believe there might be an earthquake today."

"Well, what am I supposed to do about it? People came early today — the lines are already forming. I can't just close the place. They'd have my hide if nothing ended up happening. Also, and this is a more serious consideration, if I evacuate the place, that means all these people are going to be out on the highways when the quake hits. And we all know that's the last place they should be."

Dr. Hoffman nodded. "But is there any way . . ."

The sentence trailed off before it could finish. Dr. Hoffman was staring at Ms. Eberhard's desk, speechless. I traced her glance. She was looking at a picture frame.

It was moving.

I looked at the other surfaces in the room. Papers shifted. Pens rattled.

"What the —?" Ms. Eberhard shot up.

But just as soon as it started, it stopped.

"Was that it?" the amusement park manager asked.

"No," Dr. Hoffman said decisively. "That was just a foreshock. You have to shut everything down. *Now.*"

I bolted out of my chair. We had to find Stieg. Ms. Eberhard began to shout orders into a phone. Dr. Hoffman was looking at me. I ran out of the room.

There was only one answer.

If I wanted to find Stieg, I would have to find the carousel.

SEVENTEEN

People didn't know what to do. The alarm was wailing. Employees were pulling people off the rides. I watched as the roller coasters stopped. The Ferris wheel couldn't be evacuated quickly enough. Announcements told people where to go and what to do. Most people ran toward the far end of the parking lot, which was empty of cars.

I didn't know where the carousel was. I just ran. I felt a hand grab my arm. I turned around — it was Dr. Hoffman. She pulled me to the left.

Children were crying as parents dragged them along. Clowns herded people toward the exits. Hot dog stands were abandoned along the pathways.

I heard my name called. The carousel was straight ahead of me, still moving. The voice was coming from the opposite direction. I turned and saw Taggart — bruised but moving determinedly. Dr. Hoffman began to yell Stieg's name. We pushed forward.

The ground began to shake.

A warm-up shake.

A prelude to the quake.

I pushed forward. And then I saw him. Stieg. Looking lost. Desperately searching the carousel. Searching for someone.

I shouted his name. He didn't turn. I looked at the carousel. It seemed empty.

And then I saw her.

A girl.

A girl with a doll.

A doll that winked.

Sitting on a white carousel horse.

It all came together. Just like in the nightmares. Stieg turned to me as if he'd always known where I was. With one gesture from him, I knew we had to save her. I ran faster. I pushed forward.

Dr. Hoffman was right beside me. She saw the girl, too.

The quake began.

The earth jolted beneath me. I felt like a trampoline walker. One moment, my feet were on the ground. The next, they were in the air. There was a sound like mountains crashing. Everything went out of focus — thrown about and shaken like pieces on a board game that's pushed off a table. The pavement rolled. I was knocked down. People ran everywhere. Someone stepped on my hand. I stood.

The carousel horses had come alive. They were bucking, tearing from their posts. The girl was thrown aside. Dr. Hoffman was still running. I lunged after her.

I could hear the booths crumble beside me. Stuffed animal prizes and cotton candy bales flew through the air as wood and brick crashed to the ground. Dr. Hoffman was picking up the girl. I was five feet away from them. The top tier of the carousel was cracking. The horses were knocked to their sides. I dodged poles and wires. Dr. Hoffman tripped. She and the girl were stuck. I reached them. I helped them up. They jumped off the carousel. I felt a hand grab my shirt. I lunged forward. My shirt ripped. "STOP!" Agent Taggart yelled. He fell. He grabbed at my foot. He held my sneaker. It came off. I had reached the edge of the carousel. Everywhere, there was the sound of crashing. A horse knocked into my body. There was a giant ripping sound. The roof was breaking apart.

I fell onto the ground. Everything exploded around me. Right in front of my eyes, the sidewalk was cracking. Utility poles shook dangerously overhead. The shrieks were deafening. I felt a beam hit my ankle. I looked and saw Dr. Hoffman cover the girl with her body. I saw Stieg running to me. Plaster horses shattered. The organ mangled. Stieg pulled me forward. My leg was caught. I looked up and saw people running. Hot dog stands crashing into buildings. The whole world seemed to have lost its vertical hold.

Then it stopped.

A frantic mother ran to Dr. Hoffman and clutched the girl. Dr. Hoffman and Stieg sprinted over to me and freed my leg. My ankle was wracked by pulses of pain.

I turned back to the wreckage.

The organ was still standing, twisted and scarred.

Very little else was left.

And then I remembered: Taggart.

As much as I wanted him to go away, I couldn't let him die.

Dr. Hoffman, Stieg, and I plunged back in. It hurt for me to walk. A few other people ran to help. An aftershock flung us back down to the ground. I buckled at the knee. But the aftershock wasn't as bad as the quake. It seemed to have passed.

I heard Taggart mutter something. He was buried in the remains of the carousel. We threw aside wood and plaster, digging toward his voice. It began to fade. It was strangling.

We unearthed his leg. The rest of him followed. His arm was wedged under a beam. My sneaker was still in his hand. He was unconscious. More people came. Sirens blared and paramedics arrived.

We maneuvered him out.

I stood up and cried from the pain. A paramedic walked over to me and checked out my leg. He told me I'd broken my ankle.

It seemed a small price to pay.

EIGHTEEN

The aftershocks continued. One was so powerful that the paramedics lost their grip on Agent Taggart's stretcher. He moaned as he hit the ground — the first noise he'd made since we'd pulled him out. The paramedics said his vital signs were okay, but he seemed to have a concussion. He lost consciousness again.

As I was carried to the ambulances, I looked around Wonder World. The roller coaster had withstood the quake. The Ferris wheel leaned absurdly to the left, its cars still swaying from the disturbance. Most of the booths had been torpedoed by the seismic waves, collapsing like empty shells as the ground buckled. Luckily, all of them had been evacuated mere moments before.

The ground had been opened by inches. Spiderweb cracks spread through the pavement.

There had been small fires, but all of them had been quickly controlled.

In the parking lot, the cars were arranged in a buckled parody of order. Three had crashed into one another. Windows had shattered.

But no one had died.

If Agent Taggart lived.

Shelly Eberhard thanked Dr. Hoffman profusely for the early warning. She didn't give me or Stieg a second glance. She thought Dr. Hoffman had been responsible.

Which worked perfectly for us.

Meanwhile, Dr. Hoffman was trying to reach her seismologist colleagues to assess the greater damage. Soon the word came through: The quake had not been a *full fault* quake — meaning that it had not spread down the San Andreas Fault to San Francisco and beyond. Preliminary reports showed that the epicenter had been under the amusement park itself; Wonder World had been the site of the greatest damage. Since the focus was close to the surface, the *felt area* was relatively small.

The quake was estimated to have measured 6.1 on the Richter scale. More would be known once the data from Dr. Hoffman's seismographs was measured and analyzed.

Reporters arrived. Ms. Eberhard told them to talk to Dr. Hoffman. They asked her how she had known.

She credited her cats.

The trip to the hospital was a short one. My ankle was set and put in a cast. Stieg and Dr. Hoffman were beside me the whole time.

As the cast was completed, I took a long look at Stieg. He didn't seem as pale anymore. His movements were steadier.

The Sense was letting him go.

For now.

He seemed to realize this, too. Obviously, we couldn't talk about it — not with the doctors and nurses around. But his expression spoke volumes to me.

He was relieved.

I wondered whether this would mean he would stop hating the Sense.

I wasn't sure.

We called Grandfather, to let him know everything was okay.

He wanted us to come home as soon as we could.

We promised we would.

As soon as my ankle was taken care of, we got ready to leave the hospital. Stieg pushed me in a wheelchair through the corridors. Dr. Hoffman ran ahead to arrange for transportation. I was touched that she hadn't left us earlier. Clearly, she had wanted to check and see how her cats and her house were doing. But she stayed with me throughout. ("Your mother wouldn't have expected anything less," she explained.)

I was one of the last earthquake injuries to leave — most of the other people had merely been treated for cuts and bruises.

Stieg pushed me toward the elevator. But before we reached it, he stopped. He turned the chair around. He led me into another room.

Taggart's room.

A nurse was at his bedside, changing his IV.

"How is he?" Stieg asked.

"Excuse me?" the nurse said.

"We know him. How is he?"

"Stable. He's regained consciousness. But he's sleeping now."

Stieg paused for a moment. Then, in his most earnest voice, he asked, "Would you mind if we prayed?"

"Not at all," the nurse said. "I'll give you some room."

Stieg wheeled me to the bed. I couldn't take my eyes off Taggart's face. It was strange to see him so passive. It was strange to see him out of commission. Bruises and cuts covered what we could see of his body.

The nurse walked out of earshot. Stieg knelt by the bed, clasping his hands and bowing his head to speak straight into Taggart's ear.

"Wake up," he said — quiet, but abrupt. "NOW."

Taggart's eyelids fluttered. He didn't turn his head.

"Listen to me, and listen to me closely," Stieg commanded. "We saved your life. Without us, you would be dead. You owe us. Bigtime. So you are *not* going to bother us anymore. You are not going to come *near* us. Right? Because this is a one-time deal. Next time, we will not save you. Do you understand?"

I thought I saw Taggart nod his head slightly.

But I could have been mistaken.

Stieg stood up, satisfied. Without a further look at Taggart, he grabbed the handles of my wheelchair and pushed me out of the room.

"Do you think he heard?" I asked.

"He'd better have," Stieg replied, with a bitterness so strong that I had to wonder, not for the first time, how well I really knew my brother.

There were some parts of him I would never understand.

Ever.

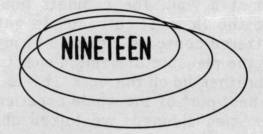

NINETEEN

Dr. Hoffman's house was a mess. Luckily, right after the earthquake, one of the neighbors had turned off her gas and electricity to prevent any chance of a serious fire.

The living room was full of broken seismographs. Many had fallen out of their shattered casings. Others leaned in weird positions.

The couch sat at least three feet from where it had been earlier; the Chronicles lay on the floor, exposed to the world.

The cats were all safe, huddled under the shelter of Dr. Hoffman's desk. Little did they know that they would soon be scientific celebrities — sage prognosticators of natural disasters.

The working seismograph was still intact in

its vault. Dr. Hoffman turned on the electricity to access its data.

Stieg and I went into the kitchen. The refrigerator had pinned the kitchen table against a wall. The cabinets had emptied onto the floor. Stieg began to gather their scattered contents. Because of my ankle, I had the pleasure of being a spectator while my brother did all the work. It was, perhaps, the best part of the whole experience.

As Stieg cleaned, we talked about what had happened. But neither of us mentioned the Sense — as if saying its name would somehow bring it back to life. Both of us wanted it to stay dormant — at least for a little while.

"You saved that girl," I said, making sure that Stieg knew why he had suffered.

"I understand that," he replied, in a tone that said *I don't want to talk about this anymore.*

So we didn't.

Instead, we talked about going home. The doctor had said I could travel, as long as I treated the ankle with care. It hadn't been a particularly bad break, so it would probably heal quickly. Stieg and I invented excuses I could make to the kids in school, who would naturally wonder what I had done to myself. I wanted to say that I had rescued a girl from a burning building. Stieg thought I should tell people a house had collapsed on me.

We rejected both ideas: They were too close to the truth.

In the end, we agreed that I would say I had tripped down a flight of stairs. (At least the excuses I gave my teachers would be justified this time.)

When the time came, Dr. Hoffman was sad to see us go.

"You have so much of your mother in you," she said wistfully. "And I miss her so much."

"We miss her, too," I said.

Stieg seemed embarrassed by the whole conversation. Or maybe he was moved and he just didn't want to show it.

I hoped that was the case.

We called Tinka, Jen, and Terry before we left. It was Tinka who answered the phone.

"That's so funny," she said. "We were just talking about you. Mrs. Amata keeps asking about you. She pounds the floor and when one of us goes up to see what the problem is, she tells us to ask you how it went. Those are her exact words: 'Ask them how it went.' "

"Tell her it went well," I replied. "Tell her it went *very* well."

As we rode in a cab to the airport, I was filled with a strange sort of calm. There wasn't any reason to rush (we had left plenty of time to catch our plane). I didn't have to watch over Stieg or worry about the next challenge the Sense would put him through. I didn't have to look over my shoulder, fearing I'd find Agent Taggart there. After we left Randall's Peak, there were few signs of the earthquake. The telephone poles stood tall and unmoved. The streets had not cracked.

And yet . . . the ground was still shifting. The plates were not at rest. The next earthquake was building.

This thought chilled me.

San Francisco wasn't safe yet.

It would never be safe.

The earth would never be stable. We drove above it, forgetting for a moment that this was not the end.

I could not help but think about what lay below.

I could not help but think about next time.

I could not help but wonder *when.*

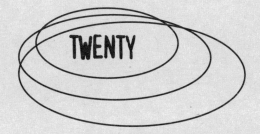

TWENTY

Our first life resumed. We went back to school. We didn't tell anyone about the earthquake. We didn't even talk about it ourselves. I think we were afraid of bringing it all up again — the nightmares and Taggart and the feeling of the earth throwing us to our knees.

We didn't talk about it. But that doesn't mean we forgot.

We wouldn't let it be a part of our lives. We wanted the second life to be separate from the first. As we immersed ourselves in friends and homework and the Maze, the second life began to fade.

Then one night, Stieg burst into my room.

It was past midnight. I stumbled into wakefulness.

Stieg was at the side of my bed, looking like a ghost in the darkness.

What is it? I asked.

I'm drowning, he said.

ABOUT THE AUTHOR

DAVID LEVITHAN is the son of Beth and Allen Levithan, the brother of Tex (!), the grandson of Grace and Arnold Golber, the grandson of Alice and Lou Levithan, and the nephew/cousin of numerous Streiters, Levithans, Golbers, and Allens — not one of whom, to his knowledge, possesses the Sense. He lives in New Jersey, a state not known for its earthquakes.

ACKNOWLEDGMENTS

In the Heart of the Quake is a mix of fact and fiction. For facts and earthquake stories, I recommend the following works, which proved to be invaluable resources for this book:

The Earth Shook, The Sky Burned by William Bronson (Doubleday, 1959)

Historical Catastrophes: Earthquakes by Billye Walker Brown and Walter R. Brown (Addisonian Press, 1974)

Quake! by Joe Cottonwood (Scholastic, 1995)

Disaster 1906: The San Francisco Quake and Fire by Edward F. Dolan, Jr. (Julian Messner, 1967)

Earthquakes by G. A. Eiby (Van Nostrand Reinhold, 1980)

Volcanoes and Earthquakes by Patricia Lauber (Scholastic, 1991)

Tremor! by Eloise Paananen (Julian Messner, 1982)

1001 Questions Answered About Earthquakes, Avalanches, Floods, and Other

Natural Disasters by Barbara Tuffy (Dover, 1969)

Earthquakes and Volcanoes by Fiona Watt (Usbourne, 1993)

Numerous articles in *The New York Times*

All figures and measurements are from *The World Almanac and Book of Facts 1997* (World Almanac Books, 1997)

On the fictional side of things, I would like to thank my family, my friends, and the brilliant editorial, production, and art departments at Scholastic. An added mention of inspiration goes to musical impresario Christopher Olenzak, who will probably continue to live right outside San Francisco, even after he reads this book.